Novelists of the American South

Walker Percy and Shelby Foote

Novelists of the American South

Walker Percy and Shelby Foote

Shahaji Gaikwad

ATLANTIC

PUBLISHERS & DISTRIBUTORS (P) LTD

Published by
ATLANTIC
PUBLISHERS & DISTRIBUTORS (P) LTD
7/22, Ansari Road, Darya Ganj,
New Delhi-110002
Phones : +91-11-40775252, 23273880, 23275880, 23280451
Fax : +91-11-23285873
Web : www.atlanticbooks.com
E-mail : orders@atlanticbooks.com

Branch Office
5, Nallathambi Street, Wallajah Road,
Chennai-600002
Phones : +91-44-64611085, 32413319
E-mail : chennai@atlanticbooks.com

ISBN 978-81-269-1454-8

Printed in India at Nice Printing Press, A-33/3A, Site-IV, Industrial Area, Sahibabad, Ghaziabad, U.P.

To my teacher
Dr. A.G. Khan
Professor and eminent scholar
in
American Literature and Culture

Preface

The present book aims to analyse the novels of contemporary major writers of the American South—Walker Percy and Shelby Foote. The need to study the works of Percy and Foote afresh arises from a basic academic requirement, i.e. the contemporary need to understand the Southern consciousness in its relation to history and culture. The study focuses on the issues of history and consciousness as treated by these writers. The Southern mind's obsession with the past is quite familiar but, through fictitious protagonists, both Percy and Foote have represented it in a new form of characters' stance towards the past in the context of the New South. Confounded by the changes that the American South has witnessed in social, political, economic and industrial spheres, the characters in the novels of Percy and Foote experience the loss of self which in turn results into meaningless existence. Since the present fails to provide them with meaningful existence, they turn to the past to seek an alternative to their present living.

The characters in the novels of both Percy and Foote tend to understand the present in terms of the past. It is because the past is heavily weighed upon their mind. The characters' preoccupation with the past/history makes them restless in the present. As a result, they attempt to live the past in the present. The past that they are preoccupied with is the 'heroic' past of their forefathers. And it is the heroic past of the South that bears upon their actions in the present. However, in the course of the novels, the characters' preoccupation with the past generates a flaw in their persons. This particular treatment of history and consciousness in the novels of Percy and Foote has been analysed in order to develop a perspective to understand their works. In this respect, the appearance of the exhaustive bibliographies on Percy and Foote, and the publications of various studies of their novels suggest the intensity of scholarly interest in their works. An attempt has been made here to be exhaustive in recognizing the criticism that precedes.

The book is designed and skillfully worked out according to the need of the students. Introduction deals with concept of history in the South, history and its relation with literature, use of history in Southern fiction and the changing perspective on history in order to have complete understanding of the issues of history and consciousness treated in the chapters, Walker Percy and Shelby Foote. Narrative Technique makes an elaborate analysis of the narrative techniques used by Percy and Foote to present the issues of history and consciousness in their novels. In Conclusion, certain revealing things about the South and Southerner are presented. This book will be useful to the students and teachers of American Literature and researchers in this field.

SHAHAJI GAIKWAD

Contents

1

Introduction

(i) Concept of History in the South

The striking feature of history of the South is that it is a mingling of both fact and fiction. History as it actually happened and history the South believed happened, i.e. history as actuality and history as perceived, are the facts of greater importance which govern the concept of history in the region. The latter fact springs from the earlier one and acquires the form of myth. Southern history to a certain extent is saturated with myths the people of the South created in order to counter the actual experience of history. The South's experience of history is far different from its Northern counterpart; it is varied and complex in nature. "For southern history", Woodward comments, "unlike American, includes large components of frustration, failure and defeat".[1] The region has undergone through the experience of military defeat and military occupation, radical reconstruction and humiliation, age-long experience of poverty and suffering. The uniqueness of the story of the South's past experience is fully realized if it is compared with story of the North's history. The history of the North is a story of innocence and social felicity, of success and abundance. The North's story of innocence and social felicity is born out of the legend of early origin, the legend of American innocence. According to this legend, the Americans have achieved innocence by coming out of the wicked old world while shaking off the evils of it. As for the story of success, the Americans have never known the bitter experience of defeat. American history is the story of success. Closely related to this story of success is the story of economic abundance in American life which makes the Americans the people of plenty. Thus the story of the North's history in all its aspects provides the counterpoint to the history of the South.

The history of the South to a unique degree is a story of evil and social ostracism, of defeat, poverty and suffering. In its attempt to understand history, the South is preoccupied with evil and guilt. The region feels guilty over its act of making the fellow-human slave. It is a great social evil that the region had intimately lived with. Moreover, central to the South's idea of history is the event of the Civil War that it had lost to the North. The Civil War was a traumatic experience in the life of the South disrupting the solid structure of economic, social and political life of the region. The South's history is a story of age-long experience of poverty and suffering, and these are doubled by the conflict with the North. Many Southerners believe that the purpose of the war is the organized destruction of life and property of the Southern people. Being the battlefield, the South lost its property in the destruction perpetrated by invading forces of the North. The region was left only with its land but there was no one with money to buy it. The South was paralysed economically by the blows of the war. It became the poor section in a nation of fabulous wealth. People lived in log cabins, or unpretentious frame houses. The region was thrown back through centuries of progress to what Savage, Jr., calls "the frontier status of their ancestors".[2] In addition to poverty and suffering, the defeat gave humiliation to the people of the South. The defeat in the Civil War damaged the pride of the region born out of its being from chivalrous race, and even put question on its manhood. The code of chivalry demanded gallantry from individual in protecting land and women. The Southerners failed in meting out the demand of the code and surrendered to the enemy at Appomattox. The very act of surrender was considered as emasculation of the South that brought humiliation and shame to the region.

The humiliation of the South was further increased by the change the Reconstruction brought in the structure of socio-political life. By newly formed reconstruction acts the blacks were enfranchised and the former white leadership class was temporarily disfranchised. At the same time, the law appointed the former slave class in government offices protected by Negro troops. The white Southerner who had pride in superiority of his race regarded it a deliberate humiliation of white people. The changing structure of socio-political life of the South had become a constant reminder of the failure of the Confederacy formed to protect that structure. The South fought fiercely to defend the Confederacy but failed and the dream of Southern republic faded away. The history of the South thus includes one more component, the component of failure along with frustration and blasted hopes. All its components taken together, the South's history remains tragic which gives way to different ideas of the past in the region. Of course, the defeat of 1865 is crucial here which gave the South a conception of the past finer, in its own opinion, than its present.

The South in its defeat and humiliation remembered the glamour of the past. The remembrance of the past, the days before the Civil War, acquires the status of myth in the South. In its new conception of the past, the South considers the Old Age as golden age and the old society as mature society based on long-established and well-formed customs, traditions and institutions. The superiority of the old society and its way of life are foremost in the new vision of the past. The Civil War was considered to have fought to protect the Confederacy formed to sustain the South's way of life. The military tradition of the Old South was glorified and the Confederacy was seen all dash and gallantry. The past surrounding the Civil War was thought as a series of great and wonderful deeds of the ancestors of those living in the South today. Thus the history acquires personal relevance in the South and so is inspiring for Southerners. It was a heritage to be preserved, a pattern, a way of life to be lived by, and mores to be adopted. This legendary vision of the past greatly owes to the literary men in the South who developed it in their works.

(ii) History and its Relationship with Literature

The relationship between history, not as a separate discipline of studies but the past, and literature is traceable as far back as to the classical times. Homer used historical or traditional subject matter in his epic poems and its use is seen in a great proportion of major works from his time to modern times. Homer found usable material for his works, *Iliad* and *Odyssey*, in early Greek customs, in practices of war and government, in marriage and in the methods of seafaring. Homer as well as Virgil mingled history and fiction to produce an opulent literature. The study of the classical works proves that the relationship between history and literature is complementary in that the former providing rich material to the later, and the later brings the earlier into focus, making the former's discovery possible. The relationship between these two issues becomes more vital as the terms 'historical' is being used to describe the literary types, such as drama and novel. Shakespeare used history in his certain plays which are called 'historical' plays. His *Julius Caesar, Richard III, Coriolanus, Antony and Cleopatra* have subject and characters from history. Characters from the past and events of history offered rich material to Shakespeare for literary use. Till the advent of eighteenth century, which produced the new literary types called novel, the use of past for subject in literature was confined to poetry and drama only. The eighteenth century novelists like Fielding conceived the writing of the novel as writing history of past; for him *Tom Jones* was a "history" for he titles the novel *The History of Tom Jones: A Foundling*. The early decade of the nineteenth century marked the period of 'historical' novel from the pen of Sir Walter Scott.

The new literary type 'historical novel' is a synthesis of history and fiction used to produce literature. Scott used certain events of bygone ages enkindling in his contemporaries an avid interest in history. History is reproduced through this new literary type in a more live way. Commenting upon this new form of literature Arthur Tourtellot says that "the historical novel attempts to supplement history with fiction, making history more alive, more real, and much nearer to the reader".[3] Historical novel achieves the reconstruction of the past while offering philosophical comment on it. The novelist tries to make the reader believe that he has actually had a living experience of the dead past. He takes the reader not to the actual past but to what Allen calls "a drama arranged by the author *about* the past".[4] The historical novel thus has capacity to produce an illusion of reliving the past, giving the reader a more vivid, adequate, and significant apprehension of past epochs. The material of the past that the novelist uses is subjected to alterations, for he achieves the artistic effect. He shapes meaningless raw data into a form and pattern which have human meaning, rich in emotional and philosophical values. In his task of shaping the raw material, the novelist can not hope, or nor does he want to reconstruct an entire epoch. He just concentrates upon that things which appeal to him. Using history as material for literary purpose, the literary men give the past life vitality and importance for its own sake. He also interprets history fully acknowledging the existence of his subjective attitudes. The discussion on historical drama and historical novel so far reveals that in these new types history and literature casually meet. The relationship between these two issues is as visible in nineteenth century literature as it is in the previous century.

Nineteenth century brings Romantic Movement to poetry and the poets of the movement treated remote and medieval subject matter in their poetry. Among the Romanticists, John Keats was one who used Greek mythology as medium to express his ideas. His odes and poems are based on Greek mythology. Keats combines medievalism and Hellenism making his poetry unique among the Romanticists. His 'Ode on a Grecian Urn' has a complex relation to history, existing simultaneously as a testament of the past to the present. The Romantic poets' fondness for strange and remote subject in time and in place made them to treat subjects from the past. Twentieth century has produced literary men who have used history in literature for its relevance to the present. Similarly these men are more interested in theories of history and such schematic theories of history approach myth in modern times.

According to Harvey "theories interpreting historical process take mythical shapes when they enter literary imagination".[5] It is true of Joyces's *Finnegans Wake* which describes Vico's version of the myth of historical recurrence. The past is conceived within a mythical framework in modern literature. Yeats in *A Vision* and Eliot in *The Waste Land* use myth of past to parody or to parallel or to intensify human experience. The works of these great men express the idea of history as conceived by them. Yeat's vision of the gyres is a mythical reading of history. His poems in *A Vision* are based on a highly schematized mythology which explains the putative working of historical process. Eliot's *The Waste Land* reveals the poet's preoccupation with past and present. We can say that history provides the modern writers with an attitude to view the present.

History is implied in modern literature and it is an internal principle within literary work. J. Morse sees the integral relationship between history and literature as time is involved in utterance of words one behind another in literature. To him history is "an ordering semiotic principle governing the presentation of time in literature".[6] History is the part of time in language. The language used in literature has sequence so that it incorporates time. Even plot, situation, character develop in the passage of time in language. Seen in this light, history is there to read in any text, not to mention the text of novel. The demands of realism required the novel to incorporate the past in its text. Frank Kermode says that "a degree of 'Historical' fidelity is something most people still ask of novels".[7] For factuality, literature depends on the past. Novel makes possible for the past to possess contemporaneity while being used in it. Therefore it must be admitted that the relationship between history and literature has been vital since classical times and more visible in worldwide literature. In American literature, for instance, the relationship between history and novel is quite traceable. Nathaniel Hawthorne used the Puritan past for material in his novel *The Scarlet Letter* bringing fact and fiction together. He read extensively in New England history to provide himself with subject matter for his stories. As a result, his novels develop from a situation or incident which lies somewhere between fiction and fact. Stephen Crane treats the Civil War history in his novel *The Red Badge of Courage.* Although the novel is a succession of a number of episodes on the battlefield, its concern is to focus on the experiences, sensations and actions of a young man on the battlefields of the American Civil War. In other words, the novel concentrates on the impact of the war on the central character's immediate consciousness. The impact of the past around the Civil War on the Southerner's consciousness is elaborately treated by William Faulkner in his novels. He is the pioneer in the Southern culture who initiated the necessity of the use of the past in Southern literature. In all his novels, Faulkner used the legend of history suggesting the writer's dependence on the past for subject in Southern culture.

The Southern literature unlike the Northern literature expresses emotional grip and power of history on the Southern men of letters. It is because the South has a unique experience of history which the Southern literary men try to come to terms with and that makes them deal with the past in their literary works. In the words of Holman, "It is the attempt to come to terms with their past that leads most Southern novelists to deal with history".[8] The obsessive concern of the Southern writers with the history of the South establishes the vital relationship between history and literature in the Southern culture. The writers in the South deal with history, often explicitly as well as implicitly, in various ways. In the Southern novels history is handled in the writer's treatment of fictional character. The central character in the Southern novels is usually obsessed with a personal, family or regional past. The character's obsession with the past has to do either with his attempt to live by the past or to understand it and forget it. In the first case, the character views history as mores which are valuable in the present to be lived by. He sees the past deeds of his ancestors who lived by the code of chivalry as the standard of behavior. Living by that standard of behavior set by his ancestors, the Southern hero lives the past in the present. History is expressed through the action—static or dynamic—of the character in the Southern novels.

History is explicit in Southern protagonist's attempt to understand the meaning of the past that he is burdened with. The Southern novels are saturated with the protagonists who undertake quest into the past in order to understand it. In his search for meaning of the past, the protagonist in the novel makes backward inquiry in time past. In a sense, he reconstructs the past in order to reach truth of it. The Southern novels in general tend to reconstruct the history of the South. The reconstruction of history is achieved through the use of the technique of detective story in the novels by the Southern writers. In the detective story a special attention is given to the interpretation of the past, and to the understanding of indications available in the present of what had happened in the past. The forward action of the detective story consists of the activities of the detective as he discovers clues which point to the true story of the crime that occurred in the past. At last when he is able to reconstruct that story, his task is complete. The protagonists in the Southern novels play the role of detective interpreting the pattern of events happened in the past which he tries to understand. The Southern novels seek meaning of history different from those of historians. Literature contributes to understanding of history in the Southern culture. Similarly, history provides the Southern literature with substance necessary in making of it.

The Southern literary men, particularly the novelists, use history for creative purpose. In their search for subject, they turn to the history of their region which provides them with a usable mythology. It is available for them because of the nature of the Southern past which is constituted of two elements; the legendary past and the actual past. The Southern novelists handle the legendary past in novels. History of the South becomes a modern myth, a collection of traditional tales which are timebound yet posseses contemporary relevance and emotional force. Unlike Yeats, Eliot and Hemingway who invented mythology of their own, the Southern writers like Faulkner, Warren, Welty, O'Connor and Ellison have mythology available in the past of their region. Myth of Lost Cause, for instance, persisted in Faulkner's novels; he recognized the strength of the legend by showing how it could prepare modern-day character into disaster as well as into some favorable situation. The Southern writers have just listened to old servants or neighbors for mythology. The old kins communicate the memories of the old days which they have either experienced or heard about. The remembrance of memory is treated as historical reality in modern Southern fiction. The Southern writers have selected and shaped those bits of history into a usable past. History in the form of myth or memory is used as substance in the Southern literature. The legend of chivalry which is the main of the legendary past, is exploited to its utmost point in the Southern novels. The portrayal of the protagonist as the Southern gentleman is built upon the code of chivalry which he tries to live by. In his attempts to live by the code, the protagonist, in many cases, brings about his fall. In the rise and fall of the Southern gentlemanly protagonist, the novelists in the South symbolically show the rise and fall of the Old South. The availability of the usable mythology for Southern writers in their region's past mainly caused the Literary Renascene in the South. History is the impetus behind the creation of the Southern literature so it is implicit in every character, in every formal device—place and time—used by the novelists in the South.

The old characters in the Southern novels represent the past and their presence is the reminder of the past's existence in the present. The protagonists in Southern novels have old kins like grandfather and aunt who influence their present lives in many ways. Although these old characters remain flat characters, they form a part of setting in which the main character develops. Time and place as the major parts of the setting have been used in Southern novels for their symbolic significance in the South. Many times the recent past is used as backdrop for action of the novel in order to show the extent to which the protagonist is influenced by it. Whatever times, present or recent past, the novels are set in, the past is always the part of the present in Southern context. It is because of Southern character's sense of time which is in turn related to his sense of history. To him, the present is an extension of the past and thus feels past's presence in his present life. The device of time in Southern novels is always governed by the protagonist's sense of time past and this sense helps the writers in the South to treat history in their novels. Similar is the case with the device of place used in Southern novels. Whichever place the novels are set in, it is always associated with the past events happened there. This is due to Southerner's sense of place which the Civil War has strengthened more. The place can be an old mansion or house, town or neighboring spaces that shared history and tradition. For the Southerner the place is an on going physical symbol of the past, the holder of memories, storehouse which has an almost magical power to attract. The Southern literature gives an elaborate treatment to the place as it intends to treat the history of South.

History plays a large role in the Southern literature; it is involved in the making of it on both the thematic and artistic level. The Southern writers evoke history through the use of various metaphors and devices interlinking literature with history. Southern literature without its reference to the South's history is inconceivable. Such a congenial relationship between history and literature can not be found elsewhere as it is in the Southern culture. The testimony of the development of vital relationship between these two issues is seen in the use of history in the Southern fiction.

(iii) Use of History in Southern Fiction

The Northern writers let go much of the past but the Southern writers at their best have used it in their fictions. A sense of the past, of the immanence of the past in the present makes the Southern writers use history in their fictions. Using history in fictions, the writers in the South concentrate upon the continuity and authority of the past in the individual consciousness. Or their concern is the meaning and value of the past to the Southern characters in present context. There is a tradition of fiction writers in the South who have used history in their works. Among these writers, and who may be taken as specific in their use of history in fictions, are William Faulkner, Robert Penn Warren, Eudora Welty, Flannery O'Conner and Ralf Ellison. Faulkner's novels are loaded with history for they are concerned with characters who are obsessed with a personal, family or regional past. He avoids the direct use of the history of the region in his fictions; his use of history is more symbolic and allegoric. He is concerned with the individual character's vision of the past and its presence in the present lives of the characters. Faulkner explores the private life, the personal consciousness of the individual character through which history is always filtered. He creates the characters who have their own vision of history. Past exists in their memories and speculations thus making it a matter of individual concern in the South. A selection of *The Sound and the Fury, Absalom, Absalom! Flags in the Dust* and *The Unvanquished,* for special scrutiny will help to explore the use of history in fictions by Faulkner. These four novels are chosen as representatives of Faulkner's use of the past.

The central character of the *The Sound and the Fury,* Quentin Compson attempts to recover the time past. He exemplifies Faulkner's concept of the time past, for him the past is never lost. The novel unfolds the nature and dimensions of the writer's historical vision. On the narrative level, it relates the history of the Compsons and of the South. Thematically, the novel is about a haunting meditation upon the time past, and its relation to the individual man. The family history which is interwoven with the history of the South is discovered and interpreted from the point of view of the members of the Compsons family. Using the circular narration, Faulkner extends different views of the past, one is held by Quentin himself. He is haunted by the past, trying to live in accordance with that past. His taking refuse in the code of chivalry is a part of this attempt which makes him senseless in the present. On the other side is Caddy, his sister, who has adopted a different way of living. She doesn't mind losing her virginity and stepping out of the code. Seeing Caddy's failure to conform to his idea of virginity, the ideal he tries to defend, Quentin withdraws into himself. The withdrawal is no longer possible, he, wrapped entirely in his thoughts, walks through a suburb of Cambridge trying to avoid the shadows which remind him of the past. He realizes he can not ultimately escape into his own private world. The tombstones, documents, and other objects from the past have the power to evoke history in his mind. This is further underlined in the character sketch of Benjy.

The presence of Benjy, the idiot, in the novel *The Sound and the Fury* is much essential thematically. He is betrayed by his consciousness consequently he does not possess any memory, even can not distinguish between the past and present. He provides the contrast to Quentin's characters as well as implies that the experience of the past is the product of human consciousness. Since Benjy has no consciousness, he experiences no past. He has no code at all. Quentin has code but his commitment to it is emotional hence lost its connection with reality. Quentin Compson commits suicide because he neither can repudiate nor fulfill the claims of the code of honor. In *Absalom Absalom!*, too, Quentin Compson along with his friend Shreve is fascinated with the past. Faulkner uses history in this novel in order to tell how the Southern men can respond to the terrible facts of the Southern past. The characters of Quentin and Shreve with their different attitudes towards the past execute Faulkner's intention in the novel. Their fascination with the few events of Thomas Sutpen's life and death leads them to reconstruct his character. Their doing it, in a sense, is the act of reconstructing the past. They try through inference and guesswork to acertain what manner of man he was. Apparently the novel seems to be concerned with the meaning of Sutpen's career but deep down it is concerned with the nature of history and with the problem of how one can know the past. Quentin's and Shreve's different attitudes to the past explicitly show the theme.

Shreve is a man who has little sense of the past. Although the past of the Old South fascinates him, it is not because it percolates through his consciousness but because it is melodramatic, better than the theatre. The story of the Sutpens family is irrelevant to him and it is easy for him to cast it out from his mind. His approach to the past is a result of education that he is having. He is a medical student and his concern is with the human body that can be described scientifically. To Shreve, truth is laboratory truth, and history, as he sees it, doesn't affect man's future. Quentin Compson, on the other hand, is obsessed with the history of the lost war and family disaster. He confronts the family and regional pasts in order to interpret and understand them. For interpretation of the past, Quentin uses eyewitness testimony, historical documents and imagination. Shreve dismisses the past in a cavalier fashion, Quentin lets the past to rule him. The past clutches Quentin so hard that release from it seems impossible. The development of the novel shows that Quentin wishes to avoid Sutpen story but it keeps welling up in his consciousness. The events like Rosa's last visit to Sutpen's Hundred and his father's letter announcing her death, overtake and dominate the consciousness of Quentin even if he has not witnessed them. The Sutpen's legend impinges more directly and movingly upon Quentin because of his close connection with his family and his region. His attitude to the past is different from Shreve's because the former has the sense of the presence of the past, the later doesn't have. At the end of the novel both dissolve their partnership; Quentin retreats to the world of past while Shreve reveals to the amusing summarising of the Sutpen story. Quentin Compsons' legacy is retained by the young Bayard Sartoris of *Flags in the Dust*.

The question of how young Bayard Sartoris responds to his past while living in the present reveals Faulkner's use of history in *Flags in the Dust*. The first part of the novel reveals young Bayard Sartoris' obsession with the past, particularly with his brother's death. He is so much obsessed with it that his present activities make one doubt whether he is fated to repeat his twin brother's demise. He is immature as well as confused so that he neither accepts nor rejects the model of Sartoris behavior which his brother represents. It results in his isolation from his family and its past, his wife and friends. The narrator of the novel describes him as an alienated figure who has engaged himself in coming to terms with the past. This fact makes him different from his brother John who had what Miss Jenny's Jeb Stuart and the Carolina Bayard had. The World War First is a godsend for John as the Civil War had been for Carolina Bayard. In this light, young Bayard's obsession with his brother's death is a subconscious attempt to attach himself to the Sartoris's heroic legend. A curious fact about his behavior is that he never confronts directly his family's past. It is only the members of the older generation showed an active and conscious interest in preserving ancestral past. Instead of taking conscious interest in his family's legendary past, young Bayard rather attempts to incorporate himself into rhythms of the land through farming, his marriage to Narcissa, and his final trip to the Mac Callums. But all these attempts failed to restore peace to his rootless soul. Just after his automobile accident, he goes to his room, picks up his brother's canvas hunting coat, smells it whispering his brother's name. After that he burns the coat and other things of John's childhood and youth in a futile effort to destroy the hold of his brother's memory over him.

Young Bayard differs from the Caroline Bayard and John III who responded instinctively to the situations in which they met their deaths as if they were merely acting out their parts in some pre-established design. Young Bayard doesn't respond instinctively to that design consequently he is tormented and destroyed by his half-hearted commitment to it. *The Unvanquished* delineates mature Bayard Sartoris in his recollection of the past—his youth and early manhood in the Civil War and the Reconstruction—and his improvement on it. The novel becomes a retrospective narrative as Bayard searches the past to recover the stages by which he develops into the persons he has become. In a sense, the novel seems to attempt a comprehensive view of historical process. It reworks the Sartoris story in which the past events are recreated in the original vitality and in the chronological order. They are placed in their contemporary context and in relation to Bayard's own biography. As a result, we get a portrayal of the past which is also an account of Bayard's development from childhood to manhood. At first Bayard Sartoris seems to be a detached observer of the past than the active actor in it. His detachment may be due to his ability to evaluate his heritage from a somewhat removed stance. But he no more remains passive observer when he kills Grumby, the killer of Granny. In the act of killing, we see Bayard fulfilling the revenge code of his society. Later he discloses that he suffers from the guilt of having taken a human life. Ringo does not suffer from such a feeling because he has fully accepted the revenge code. Bayard rejects the pattern of a succinct and formal violence, still he has taken on the burden of being "The Sartoris", of inheriting his father's legacy.

The Unvanquished presents the past in both its legendary and factual aspects. Bayard Sartoris is used as the focal point of historical process. He is formed by the code of the Sartoris past yet manages to change it and prepares his family for present and future. In his novels, Faulkner remains concerned with what history means for his central characters, with their individual vision of the past. This concern makes Faulkner use history in his fictions. Robert Penn Warren, on the other hand, uses history in his fictions to affirm the enduring value of the past and tradition in establishing the continuity of human identity in the present, and for the future. The Warren character without past is a lost soul. When it comes to the self-definition, the past for the character is valuable in providing the line of continuity. Past is wanted and also wanted the interpretation of it. Warren's use of history in his fictions is not limited just only to historical setting and event but goes beyond that. His purpose is to search a meaning for life by placing man in time and history. For this purpose, he uses history in *All the Kings Men, Night Rider,* and *Band of Angels.* In its juxtaposition of the characters of Jack Burden and Cass Mastern, *All the King's Men* reveals the past and its burden the characters carry in their present lives. Jack's preoccupation with the past is revealed when he meditates upon the word 'history'. His name testifies to the burden he bears of the past in his mind. As a historian he is conscious of the impingement of the past on the present. He is engaged in a doctoral dissertation, the journal of Cass Mastern. At the same time he undertakes the another project that of digging up of the dirt on Judge Irwin. Jack's commitment is to the past so he is not afraid of searching the human past. Doing his job, Jack reconstructs his own past and of Willie Stark by undertaking search into the past.

Jack's search into the past of Judge Irwin is linked to his growth towards self-knowledge. It reveals the Judge as a bribe-taker and the aftermath of his suicide uncovers him as an adulterer. Judge Irwin, like Cass Mastern, had committed adultery with the wife of a trusted friend, Ellis Burden. When the judge kills himself, Jack's mother tells Jack that she is leaving her present husband for she knows she always loved the judge. Her present act gives Jack the past which establishes his own identity. In *All the King's Men* the knowledge of the past is closely linked with the self-knowledge. For Warren the knowledge of the past is essential for establishing one's identity and equally essential is liberation from the past otherwise it may paralyse the action. It is illustrated in the episode of Jack and Ann where Jack undresses Ann but fails to sleep with her. For him doing it means neglecting the past companionship. Jack's sentimental attachment to the past paralyses his action. Percy Munn of *Night Rider* is projected by Warren as a disintegrated man for he is obsessed with the need to know himself. Munn's longing is for self-definition, for integration of self. Thus the past is recaptured in *Night Rider* to establish the identity of the central character, Percy Munn. Throughout the novel, he turns to others to know himself. He goes to his wife for an explanation of who he is but she can not help him. In his other attempt to define himself, Munn makes affair with his elderly cousin Miss Ianthe. But she neither has memory of the past nor has any desire to remember it. Like Ianthe, Munn tries to protect himself by denying memory. He fails to know that self-knowledge is dependent on a sense of continuity with the past and faith in future so that his affair with his cousin does not prove fruitful.

In his last attempt to define himself through action, Munn embarks on a career of violence and lawlessness. He decides to kill Senator Tolliver because the act of killing, he thinks, will give him the integrity of self as Captain Todd possesses. The captain has about him the air of conviction and confidence which Munn attributes to his life of action. Captain Todd had heroically fought the Yankee during the Civil War, and after Appomattox captured and hanged guerrillas who preyed on the defeated South. Munn sees in the life of the captain the possibility of fulfillment in action; he won the meaning from the past. Munn tries to learn about himself but he fails. His failure in grasping the meaning of the past for present living seems to lie in the sin of abstraction. For him the Association has become the incarnation of the idea, a means for salvation beyond the flux of history. History is too much with Amantha Starr, a Mulatto girl of *Band of Angels*. The fiction describes her inner conflict on the journey to self-acceptance through past-acceptance. Amantha is bound to the past in many ways than one, and her attempts to free herself from it is central to the story of fiction. She repudiates her past as she realizes that her father is responsible for her life of slavery. After her father's death she is declared a piece of property, a chattel of Mr. Starr because her mother was a Negro slave. She is handed over by the Sheriff to Mr. Marmaduke to whom her father owned money. Amantha has no manumission paper from her father to argue for her liberty. She feels betrayed by her father who treated her as white but did not manumit her. She repudiates her father and the past related to him because these are responsible for her present misery. Amantha experiences an inner conflict; what she was.

In her life as a slave Amantha is sold and resold by each owner till Hamish Bond sets her free on papers. She is haunted by the past in spite that she is freed from slavery and is the wife of a gentleman. Even her confession to her husband of her past life does not relieve her from the past. What Amantha misses is the acceptance not repudiation of the past will relieve her from it. At last, she finds it in the man Lounberry who can honor his father in spite of the fact that he rejected his son Lounberry. She follows the example of Lounberry and accepts her father though he is dead and gone. Amantha's acceptance of her father redeems her from the past providing her with an identity. The character's struggle with the past is as much common in Warren's fiction as it is in Eudory Welty's fiction. The use of history in her fictions is geared to her technique of using place metaphor, memory and character's move into the past. The men and women in her fictions have close association with the place, particularly houses which are containers of the relic from the past. They are moored to the past by the place where they do live. Her characters struggle to come to grip not only with the human past but also with the house as an on-going physical symbol of the past. It is the reason of Welty's wide use of place metaphor and its importance in her fictions. The characters in her fictions move into the world of past in order to understand it and get relieved from it. It is a way by which history enters her fictions, and use of memory is the other way. Memory renders the past. It is treated as domain of history which may otherwise be forgotten. It is a means through which the past can be captured. Using history in her fictions, Welty enriches them. Her use of history in *The Optimist's Daughter, The Robber Bridegroom* and *Losing Battles* keeps her up with the tradition of the Southern writers who use history in fictions.

Welty's *The Optimist's Daughter* projects the struggle of a daughter, Laurel M.C. Kelva in making sense out of her own past as well as her parents'. First she tries to comprehend why her father took for a second wife, and secondly, she attempts to interpret her own marriage. Laurel develops her own version of the past as something precious and must be protected from, she thinks, outside incursion. It disturbs her when friends and townspeople invent a heroic past of her parents that does not conform to her own version. She attempts to protect the dead from the living and thus preserves the past intact. A change in her view about the past occurs in a long night during which she wrestles with her own version. She confronts the past, examines it, and frees if from her chain. Welty's portrayal of Laurel's struggle to evade and then finally free the past is highly symbolic. The image of a chimney swift trapped inside the family home symbolizes the past caught in Laurel's inflexible idea of it. The bird, like the past, pursues her. The next morning it is caught and released. It is symbolic of Laurel's release of the past. Yet the absolute release comes when she confronts Fay, her stepmother. For Fay the past or relic from the past are nothing of importance. She uses the family breadboard in a reckless manner. To Laurel it is the last relic from the past which Phil, her husband, had lovingly made for her mother. From this confrontation, Laurel learns that she had been foolish in trying to protect her dead father, her mother and the past. The past is a fact no more open to help or hurt like her father in his coffin. The deads are saved by being released into memory. Now Laurel needs no breadboard, no house; she can exchange those lifeless tokens for the continuous. Laurel overcomes the past by releasing it into memory but Clement Musgrove of *The Robber Bridegroom* suffers from the memory of the past.

Clement Musgrove bears in his memory the guilt of the past of pioneering. He is moored to the past and carries the burden of the guilt of the past. He tells Jamie his early life story which is the history of the white settlers in wilderness, pursuing their dream of a new world. Central to the story is Clement's contemplation of the Indians's fate. To him the passing of the Indians is the extinction of a human race. This past in the form of guilt lodges in Clement's heart. He feels the cost of pioneering in sorrow, loss and general estrangement. Both the Indians and Clement are the victims; the former of the pioneering, the later of the implications of the pioneering. To Clement, Jamia provides a contrast in his own person. He tells Clement that guilt is burdensome thing to carry about in the heart and better not to bother with it. Other pioneer left the past behind and forgot all about it. Clement keeps it with him in the form of memory and uses it to judge his present situation. His memory of the little group gathered around a campfire and the Indians penetrating the circle and bursting the illusion of security helps Clement to understand his present condition. He comes to know that though he has gathered whoever around him for familiarity and protection may not be firm, as it seems. He understands the present in relation with the past. In the course of the time, he learns that his own family circle have left him alone, pursuing dreams of wealth and success. Like the Indians, Clement is pushed aside by time and change; both are victims of the change.

In *Losting Battles,* Welty uses the past in a highly symbolic way. She employs the recurring metaphor of reunion which can hold the past within the present. She invests it with the circle motif. Thus the novel describes the uneducated reunion against the forces of learning led by Julia Mortimer. In the background there is an old tree symbolizing the presence of the past in the poor farmer's family. The tree presides over the reunion connecting the old with the new. The tree is described as a veteran of all old blows carrying the marks of the past. The family of the farmer remembers its origin not in fact but in legend. The family has mythic consciousness whose center is the recurrence of the ritual, reunion. The circle motif is widely used in the novel. The story of Jack Renfro begins with a gold wedding ring, follows a circular path into the whole past of the family, and returns to ring itself. This circle motif is invested with the union by allying the family with the daily cycle of sunrise and sunset. For the retention of the reunion the family must be reaffirmed by the annual birthday gathering. So on the evidence of postcards and entries on the family Bible, the reunion concludes that Gloria is really Beecham and part of the family blood. Jack becomes a reincarnation of his uncle Sam who dies young about the age of Jack. Both of them are loved by the family, are taken out of circle by government. Both courted red-haired girls with mysterious past, thus making the circle complete. In the reunion motif, Welty conceives the time past as retrieval. Welty's treatment of history in her fictions is more or less similar to the Southern writers discussed here so far, but the other writer of her sex, Flannery O'Connor uses history in a new mode.

Flannery O'Connor's view of history is governed by her religious orthodoxy that affects her use of history in her fictions. She is the only writer whose religious orthodoxy becomes the central issue in understanding her fictions. By retaining the tradition of orthodox Christianity, O'Connor retains the Southern past. She attempts to evoke history behind the history. To her an awareness of the larger history of salvation lies behind the awareness of the Southern history. Her fictions prove that her understanding of the Southern history is closely linked with her awareness of biblical history. The shaping force of history is influential in life and death of man. The men and women in O'Connor's fictions are putative Christians who take Christianity through historicist's memory, identifying it with the self and with history. "Christianity for them," Desmond comments, "has become only another datum of history".[9] Her characters labor to create the dynamic relationship between the past and the present. They move from the particulars to the universal; from the history of the South to the Biblical history. O'Connor looks at the Southern history as a microcosm of larger universal history. It is reflected in her fictions and short fiction, *Wise Blood,* "A Late Encounter With The Enemy", and "Judgement Day". In her novel *Wise Blood* O'Connor labors to work out her own vision of history. She depicts Haze Mote's changing perception of history in course of time. Haze is projected in his quest that is essentially about the meaning of self in history. In his early life, he claims to nihilism and innocence in order to escape history. It is the history of the legacy of original sin transmitted to him and specified in the guilt he feels over the carnival sideshow visit. Haze's mother and uncle take the condition of guilt as the inborn condition of sin which can only be meliorated by Christ's redemption. But Haze tries unsuccessfully to repudiate this vision of history and contrarily maintains a commitment to absolute truth. He seeks self-redemption in a Church without Christ, neglecting Christ's redemptive act. He anticipates that the power of salvation must totally be contained within the self, cut off from the history. Consequently he is left rootless, divorced from the past.

Haze's efforts to escape history are confounded by both internal and external factors; his own integrity of conscience and the outside condition of sin-brokenness, deceit, indifference to truth. The objects and persons around him constantly reflect a fallen condition. The ingrained vision of sin and redemption inherited from his mother is specified in her

Bible and glasses he carries with him. The incident which cuts short Haze's flight from history is the destruction of Essex, the car. Thereafter, he turns inward to act out his own integrity and commitment of personal truth by mortification of the body. This choice is associated to the notion of body as not clean. He, too, is linked to man's fallen history. He acknowledges that he is no more innocent but inherits the legacy of the original sin. Inevitability of history in human life is symbolically described by O'Connor in the character of Haze Mote. In her short fiction "A Late Encounter With The Enemy" she shows various aspects of man's relationship with history. The focus is on the theme of death which places, O'Connor thinks, the individual life in the perspective of history—personal, social and biblical. The story describes the death of a wizened Civil War veteran in the context of history. In a climactic scene, the old man becomes conscious of the presence of death. Having dressed in the Confederate uniform, the old man sits on the stage at his grand daughter's commencement exercises and looks at the black procession forming in front of him. It enters a hole in his head slowly deepening and widening. For many years the past and the future had been the same to him, one forgotten, the other not remembered. He had no use for history because he never expected to meet it again. But at the moment of death, history becomes significant as the past rushed into his mind, and forces his vision into future.

The old man's view of history as a black procession fixes in his consciousness, and brings him to death. Although he is a representatives of history he is not interested in it, consequently he is not conscious of death. "This lack of awareness of Southern history", Feeley writes, "in which he has played a part, evidently precludes, for him, an awareness of the larger history of salvation which lies behind it".[10] O'Connor thinks that the understanding of Southern history extends the understanding of salvation history. The old man's memory of history is as weak as his body. He accepts and revels in the romanticizing of history by a movie. He sums up his philosophy when he muses on history as procession and life as parades, and he likes parades. The theme of man's death in the context of history is reworked once again in the "Judgment Day". The issue is presented in the form of lost identity in the unknown people and in different place. The problem of physical identity is feared to endanger the metaphysical identity. For the old man, Tanner death among the unknown people is meaningless. He regrets his choice of leaving the South and moving to the North to live with his daughter. Down the South the old man had enjoyed free air around his shack; here in the North the halls are narrow and dark. The old man amuses to see how his daughter, who had shamed him for living with a Negro, has to accept a black couple as neighbors. He tries to exercise his Southern hospitality on the black neighbor, but it turns out disastrous. It questions his identity and his ability to handle Negro.

After the incident of the Negro's grabbing Tanner and pushing him through doorway, makes the old man to think to return to his native place, Georgia. He wants to go there either dead or alive. For weeks he dreams and plans how he might do it. He imagines his Negro friends Coleman's reception of his corpse in a coffin. He worries he might die and be buried in the North that he wants to escape. If it happens, he will find himself among the strangers on the Judgement Day. This knowledge of biblical history makes Tanner restless. When he realizes his daughter's intention to bury him in New York City for economic purpose, he sets out for his native place, the South. He pins a note inside his pocket instructing the finder to send his body express collect to Coleman, should he die en route. He thinks that his return to the South would maintain his metaphysical identity. O'Connor's working on Biblical history beyond the Southern history is very much special to her. Ellison differs in his use of history in his novels from O'Connor.

Ellison uses history in his works for a special purpose. His concern is a hero's individual responsibility for his role in history. His nameless protagonists consider history as a means to action, a guide to securing full human rights. The question of hero's identity is also related to a knowledge of history. The black characters in Ellison's fiction suffer from self-alienation until they realize their past. The central theme that evolves in his fictions, is the more conscious a person of his past, the more free he becomes. *Invisible Man* is a superb example of Ellison's use of past in his works for aesthetic purpose. In a quest for self-definition in history, the hero of the novel realizes the meaning and importance of the past in present life. The early life of the protagonist shows him future oriented. He is eager to think ahead and is reluctant to reflect upon past. He doesn't dare even to open the Bible because it makes him homesick. He thinks that the Brotherhood and not the past will provide him with a system of belief which makes individual and political action significant. But his attempt to escape the past and begin life anew, dooms him to repeat his earlier mistakes. He has realized that he is as invisible as he was in his hometown and at his college. He severs his connections with the Brotherhood. He learns the significance of the past in his present life and identifies himself with it. He becomes aware of the fact that to deny one's past is to deny oneself.

In *Invisible Man* the protagonist's quest for self-definition in history ends in the eviction scene. It occurs immediately after he has lost his Southern identity in a hospital. He encounters an aged black couple being evicted from their home by white city marshals. In their scattered shabby belongings, the protagonist sees "free papers" of an ancestor of one of the old folks. After reading it, he feels as if he is being dispossessed of some painful but precious thing that he could not bear to lose. On that occasion he delivers a brief speech uniting the past and the present in an assertion of black human right. The closing part of the novel reveals that the protagonist at last realizes the value of history.

(iv) The Changing Perspective on History in the South: From the Civil War to Modern Times

History has been the persistent and obsessive element in Southern thinking. The South's sense of past is deeply rooted and it is more passionate and complex. The region's concern with history, truly speaking, is fostered by Scott's works and the Civil War has intensified it. Out of the experience of defeat and humiliation, the South has developed its own view of history. But with passing of times the Southerner's view of history has been changed. Consequently, there are many perspectives on history rather than one. The romantic perspective on history is the earliest of the series. The Southerner's tendency to idealize things predates the Civil War but the aftermath of the war not only rejuvenated it but also made it a necessary quality of Southern mind. The period after the Civil War with its trauma and scars of defeat was marked by great frustration for Southerners. Since the present is ignominious, they looked back to the years before the war as glorious ones. The romantic view of the past was accepted partly as an emotional requirement of Southerners and partly as a defense against Northern criticism. The romantic view presents an idealized version of the plantation regime. It stresses, specifically, the congenial relationship between the master and the slave. The upholders of this view urged upon their fellows to enshrine the ideals of the plantation regime. Prior to the Civil War, they said, their land was home of culture and refinement. Thousands of slaves cultivated their broad acres and the people lived in ease and plenty.

The romantic perspective of the past owes very much to the Southern men of letters. They presented the Southern readers with the plantation romance. Among those writers the most prominent were Harris and Page. *Red Rock* (1898) by Thomas Nelson Page is an example of romantically sentimental presentation of the past society. The romantic view of the Southern past achieved popularity in the eighties. Even the New South prophets while advocating the new creed gave their allegiance to the romantic view of the past. The romantic perspective, no doubt, worked better to encounter the North's criticism on the Southern institutions. But the defeat in the Civil War left bitter wounds in the South. Pride and hope were destroyed by the defeat and humiliation was added by the Reconstruction. Under such circumstances Southerners desperately needed a thing to be proud of, to boast of. The only such thing left to the Southerners was their past, intact and untouched by the enemy. They glorified their past up to a level where it acquired mythic value, thus extending the mythic view of the past. When the romantic view of the past was still a ruling force, its complementary view, the mythic view, was achieving the status of what Gatson calls "an inviolable shibboleth"[11] through other means. Mythic perspective sees the Old time as an age of culture and values. It was the age in which the code of honor, the code of chivalry and the code of manners constituted the Southern way of life. The Old Age is looked upon as an era of chivalrous men and gentle women, of traditional aristocracy representing honor, courage, orthodox religion, respect for women and noblesse oblige to inferiors. The South fought the Civil War, according to this view, for the cause of the Southern way of living epitomized in the Confederacy. The fall of the Confederacy became the Lost Cause and the gentleman planter became the symbol of that cause. Those who fought and die for the cause became the model heroes, the marble image, the men above men. Thus the mythic view generated the hero worship in the South after the manner of the ancient Romans.

Thy mythic perspective persisted in the South of 1920's as an attempt to preserve the old values against the onslaught of the commercial civilization. The Southern writings in this period insisted on the Southern ways of living. One of the attempts of this kind was made by the twelve Southerners in the book, *I'll Take My Stand.* It recommends the Southern ways of living against the Northern ones, and projects it in terms of conflict between Agrarian versus Industrial Civilization. After a decade, another attempt of such kind was made by a historian, Dr. Douglas Southhall Freeman. His four volume biography of Robert E. Lee contributed to the myth of the Lost Cause. In 30's and 40's the novelists of the South used mythic past as a substance for their novels. The two novels of this period *Red Rose* by Stark Young and *Gone with the Wind* by Margaret Mithchell put history in mythic perspective. These two novelists gave this perspective a way to the Southern Literary Renascence. From 1930s to 1950s each of the Southern literary giants, Faulkner, Warren, Wolf and Welty, produced a series of novels reconstructing the Southern history in every possible perspective. A study of their novels reveals that a single novel can hold more than one perspective on the past and the same author may have different perspectives as well. Thus the Southern novels and the books on Southern culture are the compendium of the various views on the South's past. In the works of Faulkner different perspectives on the past can be traced. He looks at history from the romantic perspective as he depicts the congenial relations between the master and the slave. The mythic perspective generates its place in his novels soon as he uses the past raising up to the level of myth. Faulkner recognizes the power of the mythic perspective on the modern man by showing how it can force him either in disaster or into some favorable situations.

The mythic view on the past makes place in the novels by Warren who is interested in its negative aspect. He delineates the white male and female characters whose lives are bounded by notions drawn from a remembered mythic past. In the practice of using history in novels, the Southern novelists keep changing their view of the past. While the mythic view is still appealing to some Southerners, the tragic view on history is being adopted. The new perspective is more realistic in its nature than the earlier two ones. Seen from this perspective, the Southern history remains the story of a common suffering of the people of the South. It is no more the story of a glorious past but it is a story of ostracism and tragic experience of the Southern people. The South had fostered and lived with a peculiar institution of slavery. The region fought and lost the Civil War. It has endured the Reconstruction with humiliation and lived with poverty and frustration as parts of everyday life. Taken together, these experiences make the history of the South tragic and burdensome. The tragic perspective gets free play in Warren's novels. His attempt has been remained to show how Southern consciousness can respond to the tragic fact of history. In *All the King's Men,* Jack Burden, a Southerner, attempts to take a definite stance on his past. He realizes that past can not be approached sentimentally but realistically. Southern history for Jack remains a burden to be borne, guilt to be accepted and expiated.

In the hands of Faulkner, the South's history of defeat, frustrations and guilt has been transformed into what Simpson calls "a universal myth of the human condition".[12] Faulkner is engaged in depicting how the tragic perspective affects the Southerner's outlook on his life. Quentin's attitude differs from Shreve's in *Absalom, Absalom!*. The former has a sense of past and through it a personal access to a tragic vision. In 1960 the tragic perspective on history gets an elaborate treatment in Woodward's book *The Burden of Southern History*. The writer perceives the Southern history as a sum of "un-American experience"[13] which constitutes the burden for the Southerners. Southerners' obsessive concern with the past results into different perspectives on it. They view history in terms of time giving way to temporal perspective on past. According to this view, history is an extension of the present into the past. Time past becomes the essence of time present. The temporal perspective on the past is elaborately treated in Southern novels. It facilitates the Southern writers to choose subject matter related to the present or recent past without losing their sense of past. For them past remains a part of the present, or a dimension of the present. Many Southern novels describe the importance of the past in the present lives of the characters. Faulkner's novels, for instance, reveal how the past pervades the present of the Southern characters. Past breathes all around Pickett, a character in *Intruder in the Dust*. For him it is not yet two o'clock on the July afternoon in 1863; the brigades are in position behind the rail fence waiting for Longstreet to give the word.

The temporal perspective is presented in other ways too, in the Southern novels. Time past, present and future seem to constitute one dimension. However, the focus is on the time past; it is the producer of the present and shaper of the future. Jack Burden in *All the King's Men* uses the spider web metaphor to relate the past to the future and the present to the past. In so doing, he shows how the past, the present and the future are interrelated. Burden's sense of time is the sense of totality, of the whole, the typical of the Southerner's. By this the Southern novelists remind us that man is not free in his present, and the past is part master. The time past is inescapable how much one tries to avoid it. The temporal perspective on history keeps the past alive in the lives of the Southerners. It is not surprising when we see the past monitoring the present lives of the characters in the Southern novels. Past, present and future form one dimensional time in Southern literature. The other perspective reflected in Southern literature is artistic perspective on the past. It is evolved from the writer's act of viewing history in artistic terms rather than philosophic one during Southern Renascence. The European writers view history on the philosophic plane; the Southern writes, on the other side, see history in terms of perception, consciousness, or apprehension of self. Explaining the issue McCormick writes that the Southerner "treats history through art rather than through philosophy".[14] History for Southern writers becomes recent and urgent. It is seen in the dilapidated mansions, hovering over the statues of the Civil War heroes. Burden tells us that he can see a little chunk of history right there in front. History, as this perspective holds, becomes a matter of expression rather than reflection.

History as a matter for reflection is held by Flannery O'Connor in 1950s. She sees the Southern history from philosophic view point. To her an awareness of the larger history of salvation lies behind the awareness of the Southern history. O'Connor looks at the Southern history as a microcosm of larger universal history. Her characters move from the history of the South to the Biblical history. The understanding of Southern history, to her, extends the understanding of salvation history. Lack of awareness of Southern history precludes an awareness of the larger history of salvation. This philosophic interlinking of Southern history with the Biblical history is special to O'Connor extending philosophical perspective on history. The other writers after '50s like Percy, Foote and Ellison offer changing perspectives on the Southern past. They also retain the earlier perspectives presented by their predecessors. The Classical view of history is initiated in the novel of Faulkner and Warren and it is retained by Percy and Foote. Classically understood, history denotes knowledge—knowledge of past, present and future. History preserves knowledge of conscious living for the future generations. "History was exemplary knowledge", Gross comments, "preserving for future generations what might otherwise sink into oblivion".[15] History for the holders of this perspective is a guide, a form in an age of permanent crisis. This is tightly held by Aunt Emily in Percy's *The Moviegoer*. She insists that the knowledge of history can guide men in moments of life such as success, failure, marriage, and death. The classical view of history is countered by the cynical perspective on past.

The cynical perspective views history as no longer useful in present times. The past is no more a nourishing tradition but rather a storage of bygone style. There is nothing in it worth to imitate. Its worst side is that a preoccupation with the past and its customs may make one's life empty. In the words of Hoffman, "A mere preoccupation with the past and with its relations to custom and human ceremony may very well lead to rather empty life".[16] This perspective is reflected in Binx's ambivalent stance toward the past in *The Moviegoer*. To him Aunt Emily's manners and grace seem to be worthless. When it comes to live by the past without being oppressed by it, the Southern characters take either ambivalent stance or keeps ironic distance between themselves and history.

NOTES

1. C. Vann Woodward, *The Burden of Southern History* Rev. ed. (Baton Rouge: Lousisiana State UP., 1977), p. 19.
2. Henry Savage, Jr., *Seeds of Time: The Background of Southern Thinking* (New York: Henry Holt & Co., 1956) p. 32.
3. Arthur Bernon Tourtellot, "History and the Historical Novel: Where Fact and Fancy Meet and Part", *Saturday Review* 18, Vol. xxll (August 24, 1949), p. 3.
4. Harvey Allen, "History and the Novel", *The Atlanta Monthly,* 02, Vol. 173 (February 1944), pp. 119-20.
5. Harvey Gross, The Contrived Corridor: History and Fatality in Modern Literature (Ann Arbor: Univ. of Michigan Press, 1971), p. 15.

6. Jonathan Morse, *Word By Word: The Language of Memory* (Ithaca: Cornel UP., 1990), pp. 2-3.
7. Frank Kermode, "Novel, History and Type", *Novel* Vol. I (Spring 1968), p. 233.
8. C. Hugh Holman, *The Immoderate Past: The Southern Writer and History* (Athens: The Univ. of Georgia Press, 1977), p. 40.
9. John F. Desmond, *Risen Sons: Flannery O'Connor's Vision of History* (Athens: The Univ. of Georgia Press, 1987), p. 90.
10. Sister Kathleen Feeley, *Flannery O'Connor: Voice of the Peacock* (New Jersey: Rutgers UP., 1972), p. 91.
11. Paul M. Gatson, "The New South Creed: A Study in Southern Mythmaking", *Myth and Southern History,* eds. Patrick Gester, Nicholas Cords (Chicago: Rand Mc Nally College Publishing Co., 1974), p. 191.
12. Lewis P. Simpson, *The Dispossed Garden: Pastoral and History in Southern Literature* (Athens: Univ. of Georgia Press, 1975), p. 74.
13. Woodward, p. 21.
14. John Mc Cormick, *American Literature 1919-1932: A Comparative History* (London: Routledge & Kegan Paul, 1971), p. 102.
15. Gross, p. 2.
16. Frederick J. Hoffman, *The Art of Southern Fiction: A Study of Some Modern Novelists* (Carbondale: Southern Illinois UP., 1967), p. 7.

2

Walker Percy

*The Moviegoer** (1961) Walker Percy's first published novel, presents the past-ridden mind of the Southern protagonist searching for meaning in a world of change. While the Southern fabric is dissolving, he struggles to come to terms with his own past. For the Southern characters history is purely personal experience; it is their own past, a matter of consciousness, and the hero of the novel is no exception to this. The novel is about a young man John Bickerson Bolling, sometimes called Jack, sometimes Binx. Being the hero and the narrator of the novel, he allows us to have glimpses of his mind. We can infer a great deal about his character and his mentality from the way he tells the story. By treating us to some reminiscences of his childhood and of the very recent past, Binx reveals his orientation to the past. Though the novel covers only a weeklong duration of Binx's life, the events in his past life are shown in flashback. As the story progresses, we realize that Binx is not of that type of man who finds satisfaction in an ordinary mode of living. The heroic spirit of the Old South continues to live deep in his psyche. In one of his retrospections he tells, "Once I thought of going into law or medicine or even pure science. I even dreamed of doing something great" (p. 9). The thought of "going into law or medicine" or dream of "doing something great" is conforming to the family history of which Aunt Emily is a spokesman. The past of hero and heroism stays in Binx's mind throughout the

---

* Walker Percy, *The Moviegoer* (New York: The Noonday Press, (1967). All subsequent references in the text are to this edition.

novel. He has received the heroic past as a family legacy through the person of Aunt Emily. She tells him:

> More than anything I wanted to pass on to you the heritage of the men of our family, a certain quality of spirit, a gaiety, a sense of duty, nobility worn lightly, a sweetness, a gentleness with women—the only things the South ever had and the only things that really matter in this life (p. 224).

Aunt Emily represents the Southern past and provides a living link to the series of heroes and heroism in the Bolling's family in history. Chivalry as a vital family virtue has been demonstrated in the death of a warrior in each generation. It exercised first by Captain Alex Bolling in the Civil War, then his namesake in the First World War. By then it became the tradition of the Bolling's family that Dr. Will's son John lived a life of disquiet fearing that he would not have such an opportunity. When the Second World War broke out, he volunteered for the Canadian armed service before the American entry into the war. Though Emily's sex had made her unable to work out the family virtue of engaging in combat, she has found an alternative to that by joining Red Cross as a volunteer in the Spanish Civil War. Thus irrespective of being a woman, Emily has participated in the family ritual. To Binx she is the still living member of a series of larger—than—life-figures that stretches back into history. Expectedly Binx succumbs to her "serious talks" (p. 3). Aunt Emily offers him a myth by which he can have access to become honorable and he has acted on the myth. He recalls his memory of the death of his brother, Scott when Binx was eight. His Aunt had taken him for a walk on the street outside the hospital, and then told him his brother had died. She added, "Now it's all up to you. It's going to be difficult for you but I know you're going to act like a soldier" (p. 4). To Emily "soldier" represents the standard of character appropriate to the son of a Southern gentleman under circumstances.

Binx has given positive response to her expectation and now he remembers having thought that "I could easily act like a soldier" (p. 4). He has grown up following his aunt's advice and became an army officer during the Korean War in 1951. Attempting to meet his Aunt's expectation, Binx had written such sentiments from war-front to her:

> Japan is lovely this time of year. How strange to think of going into combat! Not so much fear—since my chances are very good—as wonder, wonder that everything should be so full of expectancy... (p. 86).

Binx's experience as a soldier in the Korean War is crucial in his life. No doubt he has attempted to conform to the gallantry of the Bolling's family, "But Jack, when wounded," Lawson comments, "makes the mistake of experiencing fear, and surviving."[1] Lying wounded on the ground, Binx felt his shoulder "was pressed hard against the ground as if somebody sat on me" (p. 11). This experience of Binx implies that the family's demand for prowess had become a sort of burden to bear on shoulder. He thinks he has got himself in "this fix" (p. 11). He learns from this experience that he is an individual and not an idealized hero in a gallant historical series. By surviving, Binx has distracted himself from the series of the warriors in the family history who met death in the wars. The novel depicts Binx's subsequent attempts to come to terms with the fact of his experience in the battlefield. His such attempts are called search which will deliver him from his past. The thought of search occurs to him on the battlefield where he resolved to pursue the search.

Binx returns home with a resolve to pursue search but soon he "forgot all about it" (p. 11). He prefers a peaceful life in Gentilly, a middle class suburb of New Orleans. He sketches in the broad outlines of his present existence. He is the ideal consumer zestfully performing the prescribed duty:

> I am a model tenant and a model citizen and take pleasure in doing all that is expected of me. My wallet is full of identity cards, library cards, credit cards (p. 6).

He works as a stock and bond broker at his uncle's brokerage firm. He has no close friends and likes to spend his evenings in the company of pretty women. He regularly seduces his secretaries, though not as a practice but as a hobby. He calls it his "Little Way", the life of fornication. But Binx is afflicted with, that is variously referred as, malaise and everydayness. It is the direct result of his present routine making his life meaningless. Unable to cope with the malaise of the actual world, he goes to the movies. He goes to the movies so frequently that he is designated "the moviegoer". Binx's obsession with the movies proves the fact, again, that he prefers the life of glamour. His present life does not correspond with the one he has in his mind. He lives that life, Webb writes, "by vicarious participation in the glamour and grandeur of a movie plot".[2] But at the end of the film, he experiences disappointment. His living in Gentilly is his alienation from culture and history.

The means to escape the disease of "everydayness" is search. "The search is what anyone would undertake if he were not sunk in the everydayness of his own life" (p. 13) Binx says. His going to the movies also has to do with the search, he notes, "The movies are on to the search, but they screw it up" (p. 13). From the Wednesday when he becomes freshly aware of the search, Binx tells that he is acutely aware of Jews. He identifies himself with the Jews when he says, "We share the same exile" (p. 89), but adds that he is more Jewish, i.e. more alienated. Neverthless, Binx insists that "Jews are my first real clue" (p. 89), because they, like Robinson Crusoe, are able to function and create meaningful lives in spite of being away from society that contains them. The search Binx undertakes leads in two directions at once: towards shared consciousness with Kate, and into the past in pursuit of his father. Binx's obsession with the past, with his father, impels him to undertake the search. Since search is an experience of seeing things anew, he will understand his past from a fresh perspective. While working on his search, he attempts two dimensions of it: vertical and horizontal. His preoccupation with the problem of time—time past—is underscored during the days of his vertical search. He has read "fundamental" books, or "key books on key subjects" (p. 69) such as *War and Peace* by Tolstoy and *A Study of History* by Toynbee, terming the later as "the solution of the problems of time" (p. 69). After reading the book—*The Chemistry of Life*, Binx feels that the main goal of his search has been achieved. However, the only difficulty is that though "the universe has been disposed of" he himself "was left over" (p. 70). He is still alienated or displaced "as an Anyone living Anywhere" (p. 69), so he takes up the horizontal search which is existential in its nature. Percy uses Soren Kierkegaard's existential view of man in order to emphasize his character's stance toward history. Kierkegaard sees human existence as a progression of stages he characterized as aesthetic, ethical and religious.[3] Percy is primarily interested in the ethical stage and only that aspect of it he terms as "rotation" and "repetition". Search through "rotation" is a quest of the new as new, "the experiencing of the new beyond the expectation of the experiencing of the new" (p. 144), reposing all hopes in future. Search through "repetition" is a backward movement into the past in order to integrate it with the present. Binx is frequently involved in "repetition" or in "recollection" because he is obsessed with the past. He travels in reverse, into the past to discover new clues from his father to recover himself from the meaningless present. "Any doings of my father, even his signature, is in the nature of a clue in my search" (p. 71), Binx says. Major part of the novel is devoted to Binx's efforts to find clues about his past that will help him to understand it. He enjoys playing detective, ferreting out hints about his father. His detective work continues during his working day. He receives a call from Mr. Sartalamaccia who wants to buy his father's ten-acre duck club. Binx ponders on how much his father had paid for it, not only to get a fair deal but also to find a clue in his search. The duck-club is the only inheritance Binx receives from his father and its selling is not a less serious matter. It symbolizes the continuity between the past and the present, between the father and son. Binx's move to sell his inheritance suggests, William quotes Percy, "the break with the past".[4] But the break with his past is not possible until he confronts it.

Binx learns from Mr. Sartalamaccia against his own knowledge that the camp was built by Judge Anse rather than Binx's father, and Sartalamaccia himself built it for the Judge. He simply walked into Sartalamaccia's store one day with a check for a thousand dollar and said, "I want you to build me a lodge" (p. 92). Mr. Sartalamaccia takes pleasure in the memory of times when men did things with a strong belief in one's own ability and power. Thereafter Binx muses, "There was such a time and there were such men" (p. 92). It is the time past and the heroic men of history that Binx always has in his mind. An important concern throughout the novel is Binx's search for clues to his father. For ten years he has looked at the picture of his father on the mantelpiece and tried to understand it. There is his father along with the elder Bollings who look serene in their posture. Binx's father is not a match with them for he looks different. What interests him is the eyes of his father because "Beyond a doubt they are ironical" (p. 25). Binx perceives that his father, in the portrait, maintains an ironic distance between himself and the elder Bolling. After all he does not belong to the heroic tradition that the other Bollings try to sustain. This knowledge will help Binx to understand his own position in relation to his father's.

The world Binx lives in is a haunted and guilt-laden world that he tries to come to term with. His visit to his mother's fishing camp with his secretary, Sharon turns out as his attempt to understand his past. It is the "repetition"—a return to the past in order to review it. At his mother's house, Binx awakes at three in the morning "amid the smell of dreams and of the years come back and peopled and blown away like smoke" (p. 144). Binx is haunted by the past all these years but the situation becomes worst during the night because "At night the years come back and perch around my bed like ghosts" (p. 144). Such a haunted man tries to seek clues from his mother by engaging her in conversation about his father. She begins the talk by telling Binx that "You're just like your father" (p. 149). It is true that the elder Bolling had conducted a kind of search of his own like Binx. Mile after mile he would saunter along the levee on his famous walk. He lacked the gentlemanly qualities that were found in the elder Bollings. "Dr. Wills and Judge Anse were big hunters and fishermen and he pretended he liked it but he didn't" (p. 150), Binx's mother tells. Twice in his life elder Bolling had simply quit eating.

When Binx asks the reason, she answers, "He was overwrought" (p. 153). And when Binx insists, "How was he overwrought?" She answers, "It was his psychological make-up" (p. 154). Psychologically Binx's father was carrying a burden of the family past that affected his necessities such as sleeping and eating.

First time he had quit eating and lost thirty pounds. Binx's mother discovered the idea of feeding him herself while reading for him from the book *The Green Murder Case*. He would get angry if she stopped reading. He too was a kind of moviegoer. Next time he quit eating because the treatment had failed. What cured him was the catastrophe of war, which revived him instantly. His wife asked him what had happened, he told, "Why, Germany has invaded Poland, and England and France have declared war!" (p. 156). He packed his suitcase and went to New Orleans to see the Canadian Consul. By the time he left in the blue uniform of RCAF flight surgeon, he gained thirty pounds. It happened so quickly as if he was waiting for a war. He was killed during the Battle of Crete in 1914 with a copy of *A Shropshire Lad* in his pocket. Binx reflects on his action:

> He had found a way to do both: to please them and to please himself. To leave. To do what he wanted to do and save old England doing it. And perhaps even carry off the grandest coup of all: to die (p. 157).

In Binx's reflection over his father's death, we feel the immense weight of his past on him. Earlier in the novel Binx tells that the English romanticism, which was at the heart of the old South, had killed his father. Moved by his father's story, Binx tries to relate his own experience in war with the experience of his father. But his mother passes the experience off with a joke, making it too familiar. His mother has her own view of the past and present, she looks at them "in terms of a standard comic exaggeration" (p. 151).

William sees a parallel between *All the King's Men* and *The Moviegoer* on the ground of the protagonist's return to his mother's home in each novel to understand his father. He writes, "Jack's return to Burden's Landing is, like Binx's to the fishing camp, motivated by a search through the past for clues to a man's character. Jack and Binx are obsessed with learning the truth the past holds...."[5] The protagonists in both novels are obsessed with the past and the obsession is on the level of consciousness. In Binx's case the past life of heroes and heroism clutch at his consciousness all through the novel. And this is the reason that motivates him for his search. His trip to Chicago with Kate becomes a return to the past which is the thoroughfare of his search. In Chicago Binx, being a Southerner, sees the sadness of the Northern city:

> Nobody but a Southerner knows the wrenching rinsing sadness of the cities of the North. Knowing all about genie—souls and living in haunted places like Shiloh and the Wilderness and Vicksburg and Atlanta where the ghosts of heroes walk abroad by day and are more real than people. (p. 202)

Binx's assumption of the Northern city reflects the frame of his mind in which "the ghosts of heroes" are "more real than people". Chicago is unbearable to Binx for the another reason in addition to his Southernness; it reminds him of his father. Twenty-five years earlier his father had brought him and his brother Scott to the World Series there. Binx recalls how in Chicago his father had also taken him deep down into a building "to see the pool where Tarzen-Johnnie-Weissmuller used to swim" (p. 203). But Binx's memory of another visit with his father after his brother's death is a painful one. As a detective Binx travels back into the past to examine him closely. He recalls one of his earliest and important memories of his father. The father had tried to live through the son and the boy had refused it. Binx tells, "I, seeing in his eyes the terrible request, requiring from me his very life. I.... refuse him what I knew I could not give" (p. 204). It is the guilt-ridden "return" or "repetition" on the part of Binx by which he comes to know that he is partly to be blamed for his father's loss of desire to live. The revelation is against Binx's assumption that his father has been responsible for his present problem. Binx has shunned the responsibility of a son towards the father and this thing impels him to accept the responsibility of Kate.

After attending the broker's convention, Binx and Kate make a quick visit to see Harold Graebner, Binx's friend during the war who had saved his life. The visit to Harold proves again how the past of heroism lives deep in Binx's consciousness. His love toward Harold is conditioned by this fact; "I love him because he is a hero. I have a boundless admiration for heroes and Harold is the real thing" (p. 208), Binx tells. He deliberately tells Kate and Harold's wife how Harold had heroically saved his life in war. But a sudden confrontation with the past for Harold is frightening:

> It is too much for Harold, not my gratitude, not the beauty of his own heroism, but the sudden confrontation of a time past, a time so terrible and splendid in its arch-reality; and so lost-cut adrift like a great ship in the floor of years (p. 210).

Harold's view of the past provides a contrast to Binx's view; Harold sees no connection between the past and the present, past is "lost", but Binx lives the past in the present, it is the part of the present.

As earlier noted, Binx's search also leads toward the shared consciousness with Kate Cutrer. Her role, occupying long portions of the narrative, underscores the theme of history and individual consciousness. Though the theme is muted, it can be seen in a dialectic: whether she has to play a sweet and docile Southern belle or a whore. The change that swept over the South after the Civil War has affected the role of Southern woman in society. Since she is confused about her role, she sways between the extremes of whore and lady business. Kate is portrayed on this line of confusion and she is totally disturbed. She suffers from frequent anxiety attacks and also given to occasional suicide attempts. Apparently the reason to her situation seems to be the death of her fiancé in an accident, but on her own account the accident has given her life. Kate tells Binx "That it gave me my life. That's my secret" (p. 58). Later she tells Binx that the thought of suicide only keeps her alive. Kate like Binx is alienated from the culture and history and as a result succumbs to despair. She moves slowly to the forefront of the novel as her presence is required in the narrative. Her decision to accompany Binx during the trip to Chicago brings hope in her life. On the trip, Binx proposes her but she suspects his intention that he may substitute her to the series of secretaries. Though she refuses to marry Binx, she thinks she ought to indulge with him on the train because she assumes sex is what he wants of her. She believes that copulation is purely physical act without any moral or emotional ramification. She acts, outside the context of history, as a whore but Binx must treat her like a lady in the context of history.

The most specific statement about the theme comes when Binx and Kate are on the way to visit the Graebners. Binx confesses to Rory Calhoun that he has failed in the sexual episode with Kate. He fails because he is concerned with the burden of history than with sex, he confesses, "The burden was too great and flesh poor". So that Kate's boldness frightens Binx, "The truth is I was frightened half to death by her bold...carrying on" (p. 200), he tells Rory. What follows in Binx's conversation with Rory is his view about sexual morality. He continues that this "latter-day post-christian sex" is a sickness. To be neither Christian nor pagan, but marooned in "the cult of the naughty nice wherein everyone is nicer than Christians and naughtier than pagans" (p. 207) is a sickness too. Binx tries to fix Kate in the past of the Old South and will treat her accordingly; he will not perform sex with her until they are married. Towards the close of the novel, Binx and Kate head to the shared consciousness since they agree to marry. Binx leaves his search because, he tells, "It is not match for my aunt" (p. 228). He does that which is "match" for his aunt: marry Kate and enroll in medical school. He has planned his future on the knowledge of the past. To Kate Binx tells:

> There is only one thing I can do: listen to people, see how they stick themselves into the world, hand them along a ways in their dark journey and be handed along, and for good and selfish reasons (p. 233).

In future Binx will live by the Old South's value of "sense of community" implied in his declared intention.

In his second novel *The Last Gentleman** (1966), too Percy has shown his view of how Southern history has affected the consciousness of modern Southern character. History impinges upon the novel's protagonist, Williston Bibb Barrett, as he witnesses the South changing. He desperately struggles to hold the slipping roots of the past that his ancestors lived by. To be precise, Will is presented as a Southerner obsessed with the myth of the Civil War battleground and living under the strain of the gentlemanly code while dealing with the meaning of his father's suicidal death. Being a scion of an old Southern family, Will had inherited the gentlemanly past from his great-grandfather. His ancestor "knew what was what and said so and acted accordingly and did not care what anyone thought" (p. 9). To act with assurance and follow one's conviction boldly was characteristic of Will's great-grandfather. So decisive was he that upon once meeting the Grand Wizard of the Ku Klux Klan in a barbershop, he challenged him to a duel. However, over the generations the Barretts lost this certainty in action. Will's grandfather was a brave man and he would also have challenged the Grand Wizard "if only he could have made certain it was the thing to do" (p. 9). Will's father was a brave man, too, who felt the strain of honor so intensely that "He became ironical" (p. 9). As a result, even to walk down the street on a September morning became, for Will's father, an accomplishment of a gentleman.

The initial ability of the great-grandfather to act with certainty declined into his son's uncertainty and his grandson's irony. As for Binx, the last gentleman, the narrator tells, "he did not know what to think. So he became a watcher and a listener and a wanderer" (p. 10). Being conscious of his position, as the last in the line of the gentlemen, Will tries to act out the virtues such as honor, gallantry, graciousness, ease and gentility towards women. He admires his father giving speeches on topics such as 'noblesse oblige' and 'importance of

---

* Walker Percy, *The Last Gentleman* (New York: Farrar, Straus and Giroux, 1966). All subsequent references in the text are to this edition.

character'. He also loves to hear the stories of the ancestors told by his father. He is very keen in following the pattern of behavior set by his father and grandfather. Like them, Will goes to Princeton to educate himself and lives in the same room occupied by his grandfather in 1910. He is as admired by his classmates as his father and grandfather were admired by their classmates. While there in Princeton, Will sees a small Union monument that terms the Civil War as "the infamous rebellion". He blows up it because "It offended me" (p. 257), Will tells. The past event of the Civil War hovers over his mind since it has ended the gentlemanly era making him the last of it. He lives at Princeton until one afternoon while the "ghost of his grandfather howled around 203 Lower Pyne", he decides that this "is no place for me for another half hour" (p. 15).

Upon his return from Princeton, Will works as a clerk in the family law firm against the wishes of his father who wanted "to awaken (in Will) a fondness for the law" (p. 15). After his father's death he considers farming, but he is not happy doing it. Thereafter he is drafted in the U.S. Army—a profession that suits the gentleman. For him being in army is not a hardship until he is discovered wandering, in a state of amnesia, "about the Shenandoah Valley between Cross Keys and Port Republic, sites of notable victories of General Stonewall Jackson" (p. 17). To the army, Will's wanderings may have seemed unaccountably irrational but to us it is a symbolic action of, what Linda calls, "his hiding in the past" in order to transcend the present.[6] Although Will has fled from the South, he still keeps fighting the battle of the Civil War in his consciousness; history is internalized in his case.

At the beginning of the novel, we find Will in New York City working as a "humidification engineer" (p. 18), at Macy's departmental firm. He attends to his physical health by eating and sleeping regularly. He punches a sandbag an hour daily and afterwards he swims or takes a cold shower. For half an hour he watches television and in remaining three hours he tries to "set his thoughts in order" (p. 44). He begins his day by reading a few lines from *Living*, a volume of maxims for businessmen. In spite of his gestures at normal life, Will has mental problem. From his childhood on he has been experiencing the "spells", that he inherited from an ancestor of his namesake, and which are called episodes of *deja vus*. It follows by spells of amnesia in which he sometimes cannot remember even his name. He has deafness in one ear which is not organic but hysterical. To Will these problems fall in the sphere of psychology so that he has undergone psychotherapy under a psychiatrist, Dr. Gamov, up until the action of the novel beings.

Will's sickness accounts for the stance he has taken toward his own past. Surprisingly, he remembers the remote past but his particular form of amnesia allows him to forget the immediate past. "The engineer's amnesia was now of this order: he forgot things he had seen before, but things he had heard of and not seen looked familiar"(p. 180), the narrator tells. Will's amnesia or 'forgetting' is a temporary defense that he has discovered to escape the problem, what Lawson calls of "accepting something that occurred in his past."[7] The metaphor of amnesia is appropriate to the novel's epigraph which Percy quotes from Kierkegaard's *Either/Or* along with Romano Guardini: "If a man cannot forget, he will never amount much" (p. 1). What Will wants not to remember is his father's suicide on the eve of victory ignoring his son's appeal of doing it not. He was present there when his father killed himself with a shotgun—the blast of it resulted in hysteric deafness in his right ear. Will's problem is how to admit the event which happened after his liberal father had defeated the racial bigots. In reality, Will cannot free himself from his past because it wells up in his consciousness soon after the spells of amnesia are over.

The Last Gentleman has similarity with *The Moviegoer* in many respects. The protagonist in each novel has a sense of haunted past as well as obsession with the dead father who provides a model of behavior hard to follow. Like Binx Bolling, Will Barrett has come from a Southern family of gentleman but unlike him, Will tries to live an honorable, courteous, dutiful life, to be a protector of women, a real gentleman. Will's concern with what it means to be a gentleman influences his decision to return to the South with the Vaughts. Will's return to the South turns out as his return to the past in order to recover it, deal with it and get relieved from it. After his accidental meeting with a Southern family, the Vaught's from Alabama that know Will's father, Will accepts the job offered by Chandler Vaught. The reason behind Will's consent to Mr. Vaught's offer is not just a professional one but to play a gentleman and "return to the South and discover his identity" (p. 76). His job as a companion to Jamie requires his return to the South of history where lies his own identity. Mr. Vaught grasps Will not without reason, he spots in him "a stout Southern lad in the old style, wellborn but lusty as anyone, the sort who knows how to get along with older men" (p. 62). The gentlemanly posture that Will bears with his personality is due to his obsession with his father who stands as a model of conduct. He always thinks "father said" or "father thought" this or that and even his actions are conditioned by the similar actions of his father or grandfather.

Will is subjected to a series of memory of his father soon as he meets the Vaughts that know him. The first sustained memory occurs to him in Central Park the night after Kitty Vaught helped him through his first fit of amnesia. The memory is stimulated by the warm smells of summer and discovery of a quotation from Montaigne in notes left by Rita for Kitty. Reading the notes, Will recalls that his father had quoted Montaigne on summer nights. He suddenly stops reading and says "wait"—an earnest appeal to his father. In his memory his father is pacing up and down under the water oaks while the boy Will tends the record player pouring out Brahms from old 78 discs. His father is angry about the whites fornicating in cars on the levee to the west. The father expects this sort of behavior from blacks, but the whites fornicate too. As the son listens intently, the father tells him, "Go to whores if you have to, but always remember the difference. Don't treat a lady like a whore or a whore like a lady" (p. 97). But the memory breaks off suddenly, leaving Will wondering, "Then what happened..." (p. 97). All at once he finds himself alone in Central Park, ten years later. His father's angry speech on fornicator and lay-whore dichotomy reflects a typical Southern sexual attitude. The Southern code denies "erotic appeal" to the white woman. A sexually ardent white woman was unthinkable and was automatically a whore. His father's sexual ethic gives a way to confusion in the mind of Will Barrett as he later confesses, "I've never really got the straight of this lady and whore business" (p. 172).

Will tries to treat Kitty as his father advised him in the scene that follows the memory of his father. After the memory is over, Will goes straight to Rita's apartment, walks in and proposes to Kitty. After a brief talk with Rita, Will takes Kitty out into the central park. As they sit there in park, Kitty goes away, undresses herself and returns in her nakedness. At first he is surprised by her sexual boldness, "the astounding and terrific melon immediacy of nakedness" then he fails to love her for he "felt just bad enough—his head was caulked, the pressure turning him ever away into a dizzy middle distance" (p. 106).

It reminds us the unsuccessful sexual encounter Binx and Kate suffered through in *The Moviegoer*. Being obsessed with the Southern past, Will suffers a failure in love. In an age of sexual license, Will goes backward into an era of social and moral values. Kitty asks Will to talk to her about anything after the unsuccessful sexual encounter in Central Park. He recalls how, even during the worst time of the Civil War, Confederate officers attended balls cotillions. Will cites a letter from his forefather, an infantry colonel, which says, "Met Miss Sally Trumbull last night. She said I danced tolerably well. She gave me her handkerchief" (p. 108). Will's recollection of the simple decorum of the Old South is significant since it follows immediately after he witnesses Kitty's sexual boldness. The sexual ethic of the Old South seems a bliss as compared with the modern sexual loseness. Because he sees a possible mate in Kitty Vaught, Will decides, "I shall court her henceforth in the old style" (p. 159). He is confident that through his conduct he can transform Kitty into a lady. After his encounters with Kitty, Will becomes serious about her and decides "to take Kitty to a proper dance, pay her court, not mess around"

(p. 167). Will's seeing Kitty as a dancing partner is his attempt to live history in the present.

Will's return to the South covers a major portion of *The Last Gentleman*. The protagonist's return to the South has a thematic concern: it is a return to the past he tries to escape. Will heads to the South alone because the Vaughts have left already without taking him with them. His entry into the South requires of him, as he thinks, a gentlemanly action like his grandfather. In Levittown at Morte Prince's house, Will is mistaken for a block-busting real-estate agent threatening the white ghetto. Will looks for a fight, "Perhaps the time had come again when you could be insulted, hear it aright, and have it out then and there as his grandfather used to have it out" (p. 137). When required, Will judges the situation in the present in relation to the past; seeing that his honor is at stake, he recalls what his grandfather did in such a situation. Travelling through the South, Will Barrett's sense of haunted past becomes stronger and stronger. After the incident at Levittown, Will has an amnesic spell and he comes to himself one misty morning in Virginia "experiencing the interior dislocations which always afflicted him on old battlegrounds" (pp. 143-44). The battlegrounds in the South cause his consciousness to cloud with the history of the Civil War. When Will comes to the vicinity of Richmond, he ponders over "how Richmond might be today if the war had ended differently" (p. 144). It would have been different had the South won the war, Will means it. The Civil War to Will is not a 'remote' event happened in the 'past' but it is still going on and he is doing his best to change the course of history. At the Vaughts's place Will reads Freeman's *R.E. Lee* and the narrator captures his working consciousness and physical action:

> ...the engineer had read a chapter of Freeman's *R.E. Lee* and was still moving his shoulders in the old body-English of correcting the horrific Confederate foul-ups, in this case the foul-ups before Sharpsburg when Lee's battle orders had been found by a Union sergeant, the paper wrapped around three cigars and lying in a ditch

in Maryland. I'll pick it up before he gets there, thought the engineer and stooped slightly (p. 216).

The Civil War that ended the 'golden era' of the South, turned inward of the Southerner Will, now the fight is with himself rather than with the enemy. The defeat in the Civil War not only disrupted the Old South civilization but also made him the last gentleman. This knowledge makes Will to cling desperately to the roots of history. He reads about Lee because he is the ideal hero in the South who led Confederate army in the Civil War. He is a gentleman in true sense of the word and Will's reading about him has to do with it. The history that he is haunted by is a thing to be cherished and, more importantly, by which the Southerners can claim the superiority of the South over the victorious North. Will musing on the South says that the Southerners "had everything the North had and more. They had a history" (p. 178).

Acting as his particular form of amnesia requires, Will remembers the remote past but blocks out his immediate past related to his father. On the way to the Southwest, to his father's town, Will forgets everything, he feels "only the nameless tug pulling him back" (p. 282). When he meets Val, he is still in an amnesic state, memory tugging at him with a "terrific claim" (p. 285), and he cannot say Val's name. For the first time in the novel, the memory of his father chases Will through the region because South is "a place redolent with memories" (p. 178). Next morning not tugging but memory itself comes to Will. He sees his father reciting Arnold's *Dover Beach*, or speaking of the grandfather and "the days of great deeds" (p. 297). The memory that comes to Will this time is crucial one because it gives him certainty in action—a virtue of the gentleman—in Forney Aiken's episode following it. Forney and the company of the black playwright are in an immediate danger of arrest and Will wants to save them. They are shut up in the Dew Drep Inn which the two policemen break in. Will knows both of them, but the one named Beans snaps him on the fly with a finger. The incident evokes the spirit of Will's grandfather and father who had fought the same battle with the same people. Will, who is not certain of things until the event, recovers from his condition and plants himself firmly, "For once in his life he had time and position and a good shot, and for once things became as clear as they used to be in the old honorable days" (p. 312). At his best, Will tries to live up with the pattern of behavior that is set by this father and grandfather.

Will Barrett's action in the Levittown episode, the earlier one, is not as certain as in Forney Aiken's episode. Perhaps the time had come Will says there, suggesting a lack of certainty on his part. We mark a great change in his encounter with Beans that provides, what Luschei calls, "a fitting entry"[8] to his hometown Ithaca. Having acted out history with certainty, Will prepares himself for the 'return'—a confrontation with his father's suicidal past. In Kierkegaardean sense Will's return to Ithaca is an existentially authentic repetition which will enable him to assess his father's suicidal past and get redeemed from it. As he approaches the house, the memory regarding to the event of his father's suicide comes to him in secure form. He stands before his father's house in a moonless night among the water oaks. Nothing is changed; the house is the same as it was. The aunts are laughing as they watch the television on the porch. Will recalls that it was on just such a night that his father died. This time the memory does not break off and within linked passages Will's life of wandering and amnesia is explained. Although Lawyer Barrett drove his opponent out of town he thought that they had actually won because their moral corruption was spreading throughout the South. Will recalls his father's talk:

> Once they were the fornicators and the bribers and the takers of bribes and we were not and that was why they hated us. Now we are like them, so why should they stay? (p. 317)

Even after opposing and routing out the local forces of evil, Ed Barrett finds victory hollow. The struggle merely has exposed the narrowness of the moral margin between winner and loser. His suicide is a deliberate attempt to escape the present age of bribers and fornicators. He refuses to accept the erosion of the Southern value, which in the past, made life intelligible. In the series of Will's memory of his father, Ed Barrett emerges as a man possessed by brooding sense of loss apparent in his taste in literature and music. He recites Arnold's *Dover Beach* and strolls to the strain of Brahm's Great Horn Theme. Ed Barrett has the violent sense of honor which leads him to a duel with himself because at the core of gentlemanly code is a love of death. He is killed, as the narrator describes, "by the strain of living out an ordinary day in a perfect dance of honor" (p. 10). Will also recalls his father having told him, "They may have won, but I don't have to choose that" (p. 317). Suddenly Will feels a terror and calls out "Wait" as his father turns away. He goes upstairs neglecting his son's appeal and shoots himself. In a moment Will's problems, such as his wandering away from home, even his amnesia and deafness are explained. Now Will is able to judge his father and the time he lived:

> I think he was wrong and that he was looking in the wrong place. No, not he but the times.... It was the worst of times, a time of fake beauty. And fake victory (p. 138).

What Will tries to understand is that his father's self-consuming philosophy has finally killed him.

After the memory is over, Will mounts the stairs of the house to the attic. The room still has a sense of the past because it "had not seen touched, they were still here; the grandfather's army blanket, Pittesburg issue, the puttess, a belt of webbing" (p. 320). There he also finds the Greener shotgun, with which his father had killed himself, and a collapsible boat that he and his father used for duck hunting years ago. Will stays in the room rest of the night, "presumably", William writes, "going over the past"[9]. In the morning after having his breakfast, Will sets on to the river with his boat to Uncle Fannin's Shut Off, across the Mississippi. The world of his uncle is shut off from changes going on just across the river. Uncle Fannin and his black companion Merriam live the life of old Southern family romance. Apparently it seems the Old South world but Will sees nothing useful in it and he bids his uncle and Merriam farewell. Having confronted and exorcised the traumatic past relating to his father's suicide, Will with his clear consciousness leaves for Santa Fe in search of Dr. Sutter Vaught. By the time he reads the inscription on the Union monument in Santa Fe, all has changed. He is able to accept history as it happened:

> Strangely there occurred no stirring within him, no body English toward the reversing of that evil day at Valverde where, but for so-and-so's mistake, they might have gotten through to California. Then if they could have reached the ocean—But he felt on the cold (p. 344).

History no more offends him, it does not stir him but makes him 'cold'. Will's memory that always has failed him before he has confronted the past now "instead of failing, became perfect" (p. 359).

Will's association with the Vaughts brings him to the South as well as brings him in contact with a desperate man Sutter Vaught. He sees same thing in Sutter that the other lot cannot have. Sutter is different from the other because there "was something old fashioned about him" (p. 197). Will chases Sutter with some sort of problem for which, he thinks, Sutter will have answer. We have realized of Will that he is obsessed with his father. In his ordinary relations with the other people, Will sees his father's gestures in the people. Talking about Jamie's delaying the trip to Rita, he observes her gestures, "she set her jaw askew, made her eyes fine" and "moved her chin to and fro in the web of her thumb". This gesture of Rita "reminded him strangely of his own father" (p. 250). When he meets Sutter, Will's approach is in accordance with his own nature. Particularly, Sutter's playing with a gun and his "perky", "gossipy interest" in religious matter, remind Will of his father (p. 214). What we discern from his interest in Sutter is that he sees a father figure in him. Like his father, Sutter is engaged in suicidal effort and holds the same ethics on sexuality. Sutter tells Will, "Fornicate if you want to and enjoy yourself but don't come looking to me for a merit badge certifying you as a Christian or a gentleman or whatever it is you cleave by" (p. 216). Will associates Sutter's desire of suicide with his father's and takes a step to, what Howland calls, "the possibility of his redeeming the past by saving the despairing Sutter Vaught".[10] When Jamie dies, Sutter tells Will that he is returning to ranch where he has a date. Will struggles to keep him away from going by engaging him in conversation because Sutter has already told him that he would not outlive Jamie more than two hours. Will asks Sutter to "Wait", the word repeated several times in the novel, as he asked his father before. His effort in saving Sutter and his commitment with dying Jamie is as heroic as is required of a gentleman.

*Love in the Ruins** (1971) the third novel by Percy, is a fine example of using the theme of history and individual consciousness for the making of the novel. Its narrator—protagonist Dr. Thomas More has an acute sense of past that enables him to view history from different perspectives. At the opening of the novel, the forty-five years old, heavy drinking psychiatrist awaits for the end of the world. Sitting against a young pine, Tom More meditates that God has at last removed his blessing from the U.S.A. and feels "the clank of the old historical machinery, the sudden jerking ahead of the roller-coaster cars as the chain catches hold and carries us back into history with its ordinary catastrophes" (pp. 3-4). Tom More sees the coming catastrophe as a secular event and a part of the historical process. What prompts the narrator's thinking of impending doom is the certain signs and events happening around in present America. He sees the vines are coming up through the cracks in the streets and sidewalks. Goods and services are breaking down. Poison ivy has captured the speakers post at the local drive-in movie. Cars are left rusting in the parking lots because there is no one to fix them. The American society is polarized: the rightist knotheads and the leftist Left papas can no longer speak to each other. The blacks known as Bantus are in open rebellion and as a result, the violence is spread everywhere. Even the Roman Catholic Church has fragmented into three competing groups. Tom

---

* Walker Percy, *Love in the Ruins* (New York: Farrar, Straus and Giroux, 1971). All subsequent references in the text are to this edition.

More summarizes the situation as "The center did not hold!" (p. 18), associating the present disintegration of the American civilization with the one described by W.B. Yeats in his poem "The Second Coming".[11] On the individual level, the disintegration is resulted into the split in Tom More's self: he suffers from simultaneous depression and exaltation, hate and love, trust and mistrust. Unable to reconcile the contradiction, he suffers a mental breakdown. He is declared crazy, hospitalized and kept under lock and key for a good long time.

Tom More's assessment of the present is governed by his knowledge of universal history. He perceives history as process, a steady progression towards disaster or, a great cycle like the seasons uniting beginning and end. That is why his adherence to Arnold Toyanbee's *A Study of History*, the book in which the writer views the course of history as cyclical. The dying age, as Tom More sees it, was first ushered in by the emergence of modern science in the seventeenth century. For weeks he has been reliving the Battle of Verdun in Stedmann's *History of World War I*. Half a million died there in a year-long struggle that left the battle line unchanged. Affected by his reading of the book, Tom More says, "Here began the hemorrhage and death by suicide of the old Western world" (p. 47). Verdun symbolizes for him both destructiveness of technology and failure of modern science. As for the present cultural crisis is concerned, it is epitomized in the split between spirit and flesh. According to Judeo-Christian tradition, the split first occurred when man lost his innocence in the Garden of Eden. In modern times the split is pervaded "ever since the famous philosopher Descartes ripped body loose from mind and turned the very soul into a ghost that haunts its own house" (p. 191). The separation of mind from body transforms the individual into a "mythical monster, half angel, half beast, but no man" (p. 383), Tom More thinks. He can diagnose man's sundered self as spiritual malaise with his new invention, lapsometer. Lapsometer, literally a device for measuring lapses, is designed to diagnose a kind of second fall. It is clear in the conversation between Tom More and the director to the Fedville Hospital. Hearing of lapsometer, the director says:

"It implies, I take it, a lapse or fall"
"Yes", I say tonelessly
"A fall perhaps from a state of innocence?"
"Perhaps" (p. 205).

Tom More sees the present situation in America in terms of fall-fall from new Eden. He tells that God gave the Americans "the new world" and asked to pass "One little test: here's a helpless man in Africa, all you have to do is not violate him" (p. 57). But for the Americans the test proved too much and they flunked it incurring the wrath of God. For Tom More the violation of the Negro becomes original sin hence cause of the fall. Tom More's pursuit in the novel is for the prelapsarian harmony of Eden. With his new invention, he will help man to reenter paradise and return to early phase of human history, will allow man to reconcile body and spirit. Like his namesake ancestor Sir Thomas More of the Middle Ages, the modern Dr. Thomas More not only dreams of utopian existence but also yearns for the prelapsarian harmony. His efforts are oriented to turn history into actuality.

Tom More's response to the present cultural crisis is subjective and has strongly to do with his own past and his Southern origin. He is mentally disturbed man because, he tells us, "My daughter died, my wife ran off with a heathen Englishman, and I fell prey to bouts of depression and morning terror" (p. 20). The loss of daughter Samantha and wife Doris is a burden heavy enough to bear. Unable to face reality, particularly the death of Samantha, he turns to mythologizing the past. "Samanth's death", Godshalk comments, "seems to have been the unbearable reality that pushed More into his role as mythmaker".[12] Southerner's predilection of mythmaking is an inevitable result of Southern history; when the present is unbearable they turn to mythologizing the past. As a Southern American, Tom More conceives his own past into a particular myth, the myth of death and loss, as he sees American past in terms of myth.

Tom More frequently reverts to his past so as to contradict the present. He recalls idyllic love making with Doris, his "Apple Queen", his horseplay with Samantha, his fated daughter, and his life in the old "auto age". Tom More's life with his wife and daughter in the Paradise Estate is blessed one like Adam and Eve in Paradise. Glimpses of this happy times appear in several flashbacks emphasizing his longing for it. One of the important recollections dealing with his happy past appears in a passage describing summer evening after communion:

> The best of times were after mass on summer evenings when Samantha and I would walk home in the violet dusk, we having received Communion and I rejoicing afterwards, caring nought for my fellow Catholics but only for myself and Samantha and Christ swallowed, remembering what he promised me for eating him, that I would have life in me, and I did, feeling so good that I'd sing and cut the fool all the way home like King David before the Ark (pp. 12-13).

It is the happy world like King David of the Old Testament. While living in the world of innocence and integrity, Samantha developed a brain tumor and "The disease", Lawson writes, "presaged for Tom a fall from Old Testament security into contemporary alienation".[13] The time after the death of Samantha is the time of trouble and suffering for Tom More. He and his wife shut off their hearts from one another, not forgiving each other for the child's death. Finally Doris ran off with a heathen Englishman leaving Tom More with his irregular life. His life is filled with despair consequently he attempts suicide by slashing his wrists and then he turns to promiscuity. Courting danger, Tom More dwells on scenes of destruction, on Verdun and other battlefields. The deaths of his wife and daughter are constantly in his mind. He is a man preoccupied with destruction and sees an apocalypse that is ready in his mind. He has had enough in his own life to believe in the myth of apocalypse hence the significance of the novel's subtitle, *The Adventures of a Bad Catholic at a Time Near the End of the World.* Governed by cyclical view of history, Tom More sees his life fit the Toynbean pattern of history and hopes for the "return". "Toynbee, I believe", he tells, "speaks of the Return, of the man who fails and goes away, is exiled, takes counsel with himself, hits on something, sees daylight—and returns to triumph" (p. 25). In the epilogue "Five Years Later", though Tom More is older, he is happy having all the time in the world because he has escaped the temporality of history.

In the light of Tom More's seeing the past in mythic way his struggle with Art Immelmann can be seen as a confrontation with evil temptation. Because Art is portrayed as a devilish figure who smells bad and dresses out of style and shakes hands poorly like a man with no practice. Art knows things no one had told him. He comes to Tom More with an offer of a bright future such as funding his innovative technique and recommending More's name for Nobel Prize. Art's asking Tom More to sign a contract is a temptation to avoid. Tom More sees Art's devilish purposes, calls him "why he calls me those extraordinary names" (p. 376). Being a Devil, he has no mother, "neither here nor there" (p. 329). Art is bent upon an evil purpose such as to create anarchy in the society by distributing lapsometer and to prevail his dark kingdom. His purpose is foiled by Tom More's prayer appealing his ancestor saint Sir Thomas More to "pray for us and drive this son of a bitch hence" (p. 376). Making an assessment of Tom More's life we see that in his own persons he recapitulates the entire history of mankind regarded from a Judeo-Christian perspective. His life has a phase of innocence and happiness followed by suffering, apocalypse and alienation and then a phase of temptation and finally reconciliation with God.

Tom More's habit of mythologizing the past overshadows his present denying him access to his immediate experience. On a warm Christmas Eve, Lola and More lie in the grassy bunker wher they kiss hungrily. Tom More thinks of his wife Doris as he goes around after Lola, whispers "Doris" forgetting that she is Lola. To him Lola "is like Doris" (p. 95). The memory of his past life with Doris and Samantha haunts Tom More throughout the novel. While waiting for Moira to shower in the ruined motel, Tom More drinks a toddy and thinks not of Moira but of "Doris, my dead wife who ran off to Cozumel with a heathen Englishman" (p. 253). He holds Moira in his arms and pats, "her just as I used to pat Samantha when she had growing pains" (p. 255), he tells. Moira lying crooked in Tom More's arms reminds him of Samantha's first abortive date, which brings tears in his eyes. The past wells up in his consciousness as he caresses the waist of Moira and wonders whether the purpose of the past is to chase the man. "I squeeze her pliant belted roughlinened waist. The linen reminds me of Doris. Was that why I got it?" (p. 265), Tom More asks. Sometimes Tom More himself reverts to the past in order to escape the present. While answering Ellen's questions, he is surprised why he does so, then he tells, "I remind me of Samantha, who used to come home from school letter-perfect in her catechism and asks me to hear her nevertheless" (p. 350).

The narrator-protagonist's preoccupation with the past channels his relations with the girls in the novel. To Tom More what "needs to be discharged is the intolerable tenderness of the past, the past gone and grieved over and never made sense of" (p. 339). Lola Rhoades, the auburn-haired Texas girls and the cellist may help him in his need because she can play music and "Music ransoms us from the past, declares an amnesty, brackets and sets aside the old puzzles" (p. 339). She sustains the agrarian stability is well underlined in her speech to Tom More. She tells "When all is said and done, the only thing we can be sure of is the land. The land never lets you down" (p. 279). She lives in a huge mansion called Tara but Tom More knows it is a "fake house" because it is purchased from a gangster who built it from the original plan. Tom More is asked by Lola to come and live with her in Tara, although it never happens. The second girl Tom More has relations with is Moira Schaffner who represents modern romantic love to him. "She's a romanticist and I'm not" (p. 130), he tells. She requires a historical setting for her love because "Ruins make her passionate. Ghosts make her want to be touched" (p. 133). Tom More knows that Moira's historical romanticism is thoughtless since she is "not strong on history" (p. 134). Her past is urban-past, made up of salesman and flappers; this past is gone and Moira calls it gone with the wind, making an allusion to Margaret Mitchel's novel *Gone with the Wind.* Tom More loves Moira's fantastic romanticism so that he selects the ruined Howard Johnson for lovemaking. In both girls, Lola and Moira, Tom More looks for the "speciousness" of the past.

In Ellen Oglethorpe, Tom More sees conservative tradition. She is "a beautiful but tyrannical Georgia Presbyterian" (p. 155). Her strict observance of her religion makes her free to herself and allows her "a kind of chaste wantonness" (p. 155). She is a strict churchgoer and a moral girl but does not believe in God. What she believes in is doing right and being honest. Hester is the fourth girls Tom More is attracted to. She is twenty years old, brown haired, hazel-eyed and, he tells, "Hester is my type" and sees in her "pagan innocence like a shepherd girl piping a tune on a Greek vase" (p. 49). Hester is ahistorical, standing outside the sphere of history. As Tom More looks into her clear hazel eyes, he sees "only clarity here and no shadow of the past" as if "she's wiped the slate clean" (p. 366). Tom More does not conceal his physical attraction towards Hester but cannot move with her. Unlike Hester he has a strong sense of tradition, a sense of past and cannot wipe his slate clean. Taken together, Lola, Moira, Ellen and Hester seem to embody the agrarian stability, past glory and the saving power of music and love. In the company of the girls, Tom More attempts what he does for his third patient Charley Parker "historical therapy", recalling of the good old days, "a recapture of the past and one's self" (p. 43).

Tom More's tendency of mythologizing the past accounts for the trait of his Southern character. He is obsessed with history—universal history and Southern history as a part of it. He conceives the Civil War and the First World War as linked events in the history of the world, one preceding the other. He tells that the slaughter at Verdun in the First World War is an improvement over nineteenth century Civil War in which eight thousand Grant's men were killed by Lee's army in forty minutes at Cold Harbor. Though the comment is ironical, Tom More's obsession with Southern history as part of world history is very clear. He is obsessed with the great events in

Southern history leading to the defeat in the Civil War. His choice of the day of the year 4th July is not without significance. On July 4, 1983, he feels, he will join Washington and Lincoln, when he uses his machine to preserve the union. Before one hundred and twenty years, i.e. on July 4, 1863, the Union army forced both the Confederate surrender at Vicksburg and the retreat at Gettysburg. Tom More always sees the great historical events as chained ones and its relevance to the present.

Percy portrays Tom More as he does Binx and Will having a sense of past and tradition. Like them he has psychological problem. His knowledge of the past and tradition helps him to judge the present "fall" in Southern context. The obvious impact of the fall is seen in the social behavior of Southern woman. Tom More sees that the old sexual inhibition is gone and the Southern woman has become an unintellectual sex object. Moira and Hester fall in the category of modern free women having no sense of the past. Moira, as Tom describes her, is not strong on history so is prodigal. Hester is post-protestant, post-rebellion, post-ideology being clean of history. Lillian is a woman, far ahead of these two, who proudly displays, during orgasm a "cruciform rash" for a cheering team of sex researchers in the Love Clinic. Her exhibitionism shows how symbol of shame has become the matter of show in the postlapserian world. The very institution the Love Clinic symbolizes the failure of sex in society where the couples come to be treated. Along with the sexual morality, the other thing that Tom More is concerned with is the relationship between the black and white folks. In Victor Charles, the black character, the Old South's mutual concern and affection is seen retained though he participates actively in the black uprising. He warns Tom More that he should move in with his mother for something is going to happen. Victor's loyalty to Tom More is tested when the latter is abducted and taken into prison. He tells Uru about Tom sitting with his grandmother whole night when she was ill. It was Dr. More who came to see her and treated her, Victor tells.

Including the Bantu episode in the novel, Percy touches the very problem of the South, the problem of Negro. At the end of the novel, Uru, the northern black, returns to the North because he cannot understand the Southern ways, Tom More tells, "Uru, baffled by Southern ways, left in disgust" (p. 385). It was Uru who led the Southern blacks and Percy knows that the Negro problem is created by the outsiders but the Southern sense of community keeps the black and white together in the South.

*Lancelot** (1971), the fourth novel by Percy, describes the title character's obsession with the ancestral past as mores, and his fury at the collapse of values in the modern times, specified by sexual betrayal and bribery within the family. Being the scion of a Southern family of gentlemen, the protagonist Lancelot Andrewes Lamar has a sense of honor as a property of hereditary social status that his family enjoys "as an enclave of the English gentry" (p. 14). When the later members of the Lamar family do not maintain the social status, he becomes violent to restore it. In a sense, the character of Lancelot is a good example of the Southern mind closed within history and is ever ready to act it out when situation demands. The primary focus of the novel, thus, is on the past-ridden consciousness of Lancelot, which affects everything he does in the present. In order to examine the issue of history and individual consciousness, it is necessary to refer to the Lamar family heritage that has formative influence on Lancelot's character. The Lamars have been a noble family in the South for its members lived by the code of chivalry. Lancelot's great-grandfather Manson Maury Lamar fought under the command of Lee in the Civil War "on the bloodiest day of the war" (p. 217). The same ancestor had had a duel with a man who questioned his blood relationship saying that his mother, a white Creol lady, had had sexual relations with a Negro. The ancestor had cut the throat of the man, setting an example of

---

* Walker Percy, *Lancelot* (New York: Farrar, 1977). All subsequent references in the text are to this edition.

defending family blood, which in turn was defending honor by violence.

In the later generation of the Lamar family, Lancelot's uncle keeps himself with the family tradition by fighting in the Argonne in the First World War. Lancelot grows up on the line of the family heritage with a repressed need for performing something courageous or heroic. He defends the Buells, a slave family, and their black Baptist church from the local Kluxer who threatened them to kill and destroy their church. Following up the soldierly tradition of the family, Lancelot joins the army but he cannot stay longer there because he "is discharged from the army not bloody and victorious and battered" but "with persistent diarrhea" (p. 28). When Lancelot was a student of Southern history, he studied the history of the Civil War with a religious fervor and thought Lee as a patron saint of the region. The influence of the past tradition on Lancelot's character is felt in his attitude towards life. He thinks of women either a lady or a whore, as his ancestor did, and one could consort with whore but marry a lady. He marries Lucy Cobb of Georgia, because she is an ideal type that he dreams of; "Lucy was a virgin! and I did not want her otherwise" (p. 85), he tells. His relations with Margot, his second wife, are governed by this romantic-idealist view of women. It is made clear by Margot herself in her last words with Lancelot before she is burned in the fire of Belle Isle. She tells him, "With you I had to be either—or—but never a—uh—woman" (p. 245).

Although Margot comes from west Texas, she has been posing herself as a Southern belle the day both she and Lancelot have meet at Belle Isle. She charms him with her first words, "You must be the master" (p. 73). In the early days of their marriage, it is Margot who encourages Lancelot to identify himself with the Old South figures. Restoring Belle Isle to its pre-war splendor, Margot puts a plantation desk and chair in Lancelot's study room for turning him "into Jefferson Davis writing his memoirs" (p. 82). In order to revive the past, she insists her husband to drink toddies and juleps and wear linen suits. Lancelot's mute consent to Margot's attempts of restoring the mansion and its master to the past glory is understandable enough in relations to his obsession with the past.

The central action of the novel *Lancelot*, in fact, is Lancelot's desperate attempt to defend "the grand mythic Lamar tradition" (p. 92). As the central character, he puts the novel in action soon as he discovers Siobhan's, his daughter's blood type not corresponding with his own blood type. The discovery of incompatibility of blood type creates a "worm of interest" in Lancelot that carries him into the root of the matter. He ponders over the possible blood type of Siobhan from the equations of his blood type with Margot's. To be sure, Lancelot consults with a physician, his cousin, and learns from him that his blood type cannot beget a type 'O' that is his daughter's. Still hanging upon the problem, Lancelot comes to know the possible time when Siobhan was conceived by subtracting two hundred and eighty days from her birthday, April 21, 1969. From the past documents and calculations, Lancelot learns that in the year 1968 Margot was in Texas at Bob Merlin's acting workshop for the entire month of July during which Siobhan must have been conceived. It is clear that Margot committed adultery in 1968, and the proof of which was a daughter who possessed a blood type not determined by her father's. Lancelot's meticulous act of pursuing the truth of his daughter's blood type exhibits an intensely Southern obsession with blood relationship that decides one's status in society.

The discovery of Margot's infidelity reminds Lancelot of the discovery of his father's bribery and also his mother's possible affair with uncle Harry. Lancelot's father was accused of taking the kickback money from the crooked politician but the Lamar family denied the accusation thinking that it was the "usual story of the honorable man besmirched by dirty politicians" (p. 41). Aftermath of the accusation—denial period, the child Lancelot discovers some ten thousand dollars in his father's sock drawer while searching for ten dollar for his mother's shopping. The sudden discovery of money confirms Lancelot's father being a crook and for Lancelot the "old world fell to pieces" at the sight of money (p. 42). The worst follows, Lancelot's father, demoralized, retires from the world into a fantasy of Southern romanticism leaving his wife Lily to a distant relative called uncle Harry. Lancelot recalls how his father asks uncle Harry to take Lily for "joyrides", "Get her out of the house, Harry!" my father said—leaving him, my father, to his beloved quiet" (p. 215), Lancelot tells. Lancelot's belief in his father's sexual failure and his mother's possible love affair with uncle Harry is made certain by a woman in a hallucination before he kills Jacoby. The woman, whom Lancelot calls "Our Lady of the Camellias", tells him that his mother and Uncle Harry were lovers. Lancelot draws a comparison between his father's corruption and sexual failure, and Margot's infidelity concluding that in both cases the members of the family have failed to live up to the traditional moral code—rule of honor.

Lancelot's actions after the discovery of his wife's adultery is conditioned by the sense of lost honor which almost drives him mad. He oscillates between two different views of his wife's infidelity. His first view, shaped by the scientific mind, sees "Margot's fornication, anybody's fornication, amounts to no more than molecules encountering molecules" (p. 89). This view reveals that sexual act has nothing to do with honor and performing it, no honor is spoiled. Lancelot's other view, shaped by the heroic tradition, sees Margot's sexual relations outside the marriage as a blow to the moral code and hence unforgivable. The later view prevails and Lancelot will retrieve the lost honor in a way his ancestor had done in the past. Lancelot prefers the old style of life because for him it is the only way to live by in modern Sodom; "I could live that way, crude as it was.... But it is at least a way to live" (p. 155), he tells. The old code demands violent action against the culprits but one must be sure of oneself before doing it. That is why Lancelot tells, "I had to be absolutely certain" (p. 43) of what Margot has done and is doing now. He undertakes a quest leading to the truth of his wife's infidelity by the way of spotting her in the bed with her lover. In other respect, Lancelot thinks, the search will reveal him a "sin" or an "evil" which is necessary to prove the existence of God. He calls himself the knight of the Unholy Grail and sexual sin is the "Unholy Grail" he seeks. He knows that his search is peculiar but peculiar time needs peculiar search. Lancelot's sense of sin reflects Southern writer's common tendency that has its source in the region's history in which one race did injustice on the other by enslaving it.

Lancelot's quest is rightly understood as his romantic obsession with the heroic ideal which is sprung from his honor-conscious feeling of jealousy. He is single minded in his pursuit of the exposure of his wife with her lover whom he still assumes to be Merlin. In his search, Lancelot seeks help from Elgin, the most trusted black servant, whom he asks to keep a log of the film crews activities in the Holiday Inn where they are staying. What he asks from Elgin is note of "what a person may carry with him, what they do, the smallest item of behavior" (p. 98). Lancelot infers from the log kept by Elgin the only possibility that Margot might lust for someone not him. The next step in his quest is to film, by using hidden camera in the rooms, Margot and her lover making love. For this commission there is no better man than Elgin who has technical competence and can be trusted absolutely too. The movie made by him exposes the fact that Margot has two lovers, Merlin the ex-lover and Jacoby the present lover. Being certain, now, about his wife's infidelity that is the prerequisite for violent action, Lancelot makes preparation to avenge his honor. In the action against the culprits the innocents must be spared so that Lancelot sends Tex and Siobhan away and surprisingly, asks Merlin to leave the place. Lancelot forces Lucy who wishes to stay with Rain to go to school. His manner of acting out of certainty impresses the people around there who "acted as if I were an ancestor who had wandered out of his portrait and begun giving orders" (p. 205), he tells. Lancelot's pose for an ancestor surprises Lucy who asks Suellen, "What's got into Papa?" (p. 205).

Lancelot's act of killing Jacoby and Margot is replica of the past example of using violence for defending honor. He arms with a bowie knife, supposed to be one of Bowie original, and walks in on the bed where Jacoby and Margot are making love. He takes fight with Jacoby, holds him and cuts his throat in the same manner as the Lamar ancestor had cut the throat of his adversary. History is acted out in the present. Lancelot retrieves his lost honor by using violence in the grand Lamar tradition. It is an act of a Southern mind pregnant with history controlling the person who possess it. Lancelot performs the 'great deed' of defending honor in the killing of Jacoby and Margot in the traditional sense, but there is a discord with the tradition. He lacks the great feeling—of anger, joy, revenge— as he was taught to have to match the great deed being performed. He performs the great act without having such feeling; "I remember casting about for the feeling and not finding one" (p. 242), Lancelot admits. In a sense, it is an attempt on the part of Lancelot of keeping distance between himself and the act performed. Even years after when he looks at the past incident he feels "nothing...except a certain coldness" (p. 253).

The quest that Lancelot has undertaken to find evil in the sexual act between Margot and her lover is failed because he finds nothing there except the "beastliness" of the act. After the failure of the quest, Lancelot rejects the present age calling it the "the great whorehouse and fagdom of America" (p. 176) which hits his wife, daughter, son and mother. With the burning of the Belle Isle symbolizing the past, Lancelot, what Sweeny calls, "has literally blown away his own past".[14] Burning the past and rejecting the present, Lancelot will start afresh initiating a new order in the Shenandoah Valley, the old womblike seat of Southern glory and defeat. The new society will be based on the codes of courtesy and chivalry, the codes the noble men of the past lived by. In the new order, Lancelot tells, "there will be tight-lipped courtesy between men. And chivalry toward women", because "women must be saved from the whoredom they've chosen" (p. 58). And women shall be treated as either ladies or whores. Anna the gang-raped girl must be the new woman and Lancelot be the new man in the new society, because, he tells, they "were suited to each other, each stripped of the past" (p. 250). Though Lancelot talks of starting off a new order of things, he ends with repeating a good many aspects of the worn-out past revealing his preoccupation with Southern history. His vision of a new age bears a strong resemblance to the old, mythic Southern past. But Lancelot denies any such resemblance, "Don't confuse it with anything you've heard of before" (p. 156), he warns. In his idea of a new society populated with chivalrous, violent men quick to defend honor, and women being categorized as either ladies or whores, we hear an echo of the old South tradition. Lancelot's disgust with the modern world of corruption and adultery makes him plan a new society based on stoic values without knowing it.

Lancelot's preoccupation with history is presented in his attempts to understand the time—time past, present and future. As a part of his habit, he sees things in terms of time, for example, he corresponds the three stages of his life with the divisions of time into three periods. The first period he calls Romantic Period when one falls in love; the next is a sexual period in which men and women cohabit as indiscriminately as in a soap opera; the third is a period of catastrophe. There is a Romantic Period in Lancelot's life when he falls in love with Margot; it is followed by a sexual period when Margot lusts for other men; there is a period of catastrophe when Lancelot burns the Belle Isle with his wife. Even his idea of the divisions of time is a part of his sexual theory of history which in turn born out of his sexual hang-up caused by Margot's adultery. After the period of catastrophe, Lancelot foresees a new order that he calls 'The Third Revolution' patterning his idea in the course of American history. The course of American history begins with the First Revolution won against the Britishers in 1776 through the Second Revolution—the Civil War—lost against "the money-grubbing" North. And Lancelot's Third Revolution "will begin in the wilderness where Lee lost" (p. 158).

The discovery of Margot's infidelity is a great blow to Lancelot's concept of time. The very thought of his wife loving the other man the way she once loved him arouses jealousy in Lancelot. To him "Jealousy is an alteration in the very shape of time itself. Time loses its structure" (p. 122). Time is altered; what was good time for Lancelot is changed into bad one. In original structure, the time present is an extension of the time past into the time future. But in its altered form, time present bears no relation with the time past. Lancelot tells that his and Margot's "great locker-room lust had no relation to the present. Lust is a function of the future (p. 235). Time and again Lancelot tells us his problem with time and his attempts to deal with it. To him to live in the past and future is not a problem but to live in present is not easy. "To live in the past and future is easy. To live in the present is like threading a needle" (p. 235), Lancelot tells. In this respect Lancelot's actions in the novel can be seen as his attempt to set the time in order.

Year after the incident at the Belle Isle Lancelot is unwilling to even remember the past because he is sure "that the past is absolutely dead" (p. 62). Instead he looks forward to the future that is "absolutely new". What is the more of the past is, he confides to Percival, that the past is intolerable "just because it is so goddamn banal and feckless and useless" (p. 105).

Lancelot tries to come to terms with the intolerable past in order to have the pure future. He is aware that "the passage of time is nothing but the encroachment of the horrible banality of the past on the pure future" (p. 106). To endure the horrible banality of the past, Lancelot has to find a clue that he missed in the past. In other words, the past holds knowledge and Lancelot has to unravel it, "so" he tells, "I won't make the same mistake twice" (p. 108).

As do the earlier novels of Percy, his fifth novel, *The Second Coming** (1980), explores the theme of history and individual consciousness with its central character Willistom Bibb Barrett increasingly obsessed with his past. Returning to the character of Will Barrett that he has left at the close of *The Last Gentleman*, Percy projects him in his middle forties as yet

---

* Walker Percy, *The Second Coming* (New York: Farrar, Giroux, 1980). All subsequent references in the text are to this edition.

still plagued by memories from the past that make it impossible for him to live in the present. He is not of the present and at the outset of the novel the narrator draws our attention to his characteristic illness and to his mental make up. He is feeling depressed and is subjected to "spells"—"petty—mall trance" (p. 11), doctor calls them. He thinks life more senseless, even demented and the world to him has become farcical. He inquires the doctor whether the tendency to suicide is inherited while entertaining the thought of shooting himself. He does fall down as well as he remembers everything, a symptom the narrator describes is "the opposite amnesia" (p. 9). He muses on the apocalypse for the Jews have returned to Israel that he takes a sure sign of the second coming of Christ is at hand. Taken together, the illness of Will Barrett accounts for the state of alienation that Soren Kierkegaard describes and Percy uses it to view his character from existential perspective. To explore why Will Barrett senses the end of his life and the world, it is necessary to examine his past or his relationship with the past.

The Second Coming depicts the protagonist's relationship with his dark past relating to his father's suicide. The past is called back into his consciousness since. "Everything reminded him of something else" (p. 9). Lying in the bunker on the golf course at the Linwood Country Club on an ordinary October afternoon in North Carolina, he hears a sound that reminds him of an important event in the distant past which "he had managed until that moment to forget it" (p. 3). Will Barrett is not willing to recall and still is overtaken by the memories of the past because they are "memories of extraordinary power and poignancy" (p. 12). The memories now intrude upon Will Barrett's consciousness are of the hunting trip with his father to Thomasville, Georgia, thirty years before when he was a boy. The event on the hunting trip is significant to Will Barrett for it is the only event that "ever happened to him in his life", other that happened afterwards is "non-event" (p. 52). It is that event which is pregnant with meanings that he longs to know and still its memory that he wants to escape from.

Throughout the novel, Will Barrett is haunted by his past owing to his conditions of total recall of the past. The memory that visits him, brings with it the knowledge of the present. The narrator acutely puts it that "at the very moment of his remembering the distant past, the meaning of his present life became clear to him" (p. 71). Now Will Barrett realizes that he always wanted to get rid of his past related to his father and all that his father stands for. In one of his mental colloquies with the father, he admits the fact:

> Ever since your death, all I ever wanted from you was out, out from you...out from the ancient hatred and allegiances, allegiances unto death and love of war and rumors of war.... (p. 72).

To escape the past, Will Barrett runs away from the South to the North. He runs after love, money and little Christianity. He marries Marion, the only daughter of wealthy Peabody; becomes a successful Wall Street lawyer. After Marion's death, he inherits her fortune, retires early and returns to live on his ten thousand acres of mountainside in Linwood, North Carolina. Lately, he has been named Rotary's Man-of-the year for his service to the community. Now as he remembers the distant past his successful Yankee life of thirty years in the North seems to him "a long night's dream" (p. 73). At the same time he realized that he cannot evade the memory of the past, "after all", he tells his father, "no escaping it for us" (p. 73).

The memory of the past rushing into Will Barrett's mind and his relentlessly probing it, have been central to the texture of the novel. Many times the memories of the past flood his consciousness, each time he tries to grab meanings from them. What he tries to discern from the memories is that what actually happened on the hunting trip and why his father later killed himself. Trying again and again, Will Barrett finally penetrates into the obscurity of the event on the hunting trip. In his memory, now at this time, he clearly sees that just after the cursing at the fence and just before an unsuccessful suicide attempt, his father had attempted to kill him, Will Barrett. Those two blasts from the father's shotgun, which everyone said had been intended for the single quail in the brush, had actually been intended for Will Barrett himself. The scars on his cheek are visible signs of the wounding, physical and psychic, that he received from his father. In the event, there is a steady, awful escalation of the father's violence towards the son; first the curse, then the father's suicide attempt and the father's attempt to kill the son. Will Barrett's analysis of the past is essentially an attempt to understand his father and his frame of mind. Seen from this perspective, the two interrelated incidents, the father's suicide and his attempt to kill his son cannot be understood without relating them to the Southern Stoicism that the father had imbibed.

The Stoical view perceives that the virtues of truth and courage and honor are inevitably doomed to defeat at the hands of unworthy masses. To emphasize the father's Stoical frame of mind Percy has Will Barrett recall his father discussing the present state of existence one evening during Eisenhower years. Trying to describe the present state of living, the father fumbles for a word to describe it. "What is the word for a state", the father asks, "which is not life and not death, a death in life?" (p. 126). He even wonders if such a time happened in history before. The only cure for the malady of the present times is war; for the father war counters the death-in-life state. When the Second World War breaks out, the father enters the war with a great joy; when peace follows, he becomes unhappy. The things he brings home from the war are the most prized possessions to him; they include a German Luger, an officer's hat, and some photographs he removed from the body of a dead German soldier. These things remind him of the honor and gallantry of war in a world that lacks them. Interestingly, the father, as Will Barrett remembers, never mentioned the horrors he witnessed at Buchenwald.

The father's dissatisfaction with the present existence extends to his world of hunting. He is not happy with the results of the present hunting in comparison with the past hunting. The father and grandfather had a great hunt here when the father was a boy, but now there is a falling off. Now the guide is poor, the dog is untrained and even the hotel is not as good as the father remembered from his trip. The old items are always better in every important way in the father's memory. In his search to know his father, Will Barrett realizes that the father was dissatisfied with the world and loved war for death. Underlying these two traits—dissatisfaction and love of war—is anger that motivated the father to suicide. Will Barrett recalls how the father knew by heart a letter by Marcus Flavinius, a Roman centurion, who had imbibed the Stoicism of the Empire. Hearing that corruption and decay were rampant in Rome, Marcus sounded a warning, "beware of the anger of the Legions" (p. 133). This memory brings forth the crucial trait of the father-anger, "You were possessed by anger", Will Barrett tells the father, "anger which in the end you turn yourself" (p. 133).

Not just the anger, but the sudden anger was characteristic of the father is perceived by Ewell McBee, a childhood friend to Will Barrett. He tells Will Barrett how his father, once, "was getting hot under the collar" (p. 175) while listening to a preacher who kept on talking about church, money and saving soul. Then he tells how the father told the preacher about the soul, about the man in an abusive language and ultimately Ewell tells Will Barrett, "I'm telling you, your daddy was a pistol-ball" (p. 176). The father was consumed by sudden anger that was appeased with his suicide. Intimately related to the anger is the Southern code of honor. The father suffers a sense of lost honor as does Jim in *Lord Jim* by Conrad, the novel the father reads and the son saves it for himself. Will Barrett tells how his father "had the guilts like Jim and an enemy he hated, himself" (p. 146). Honor, melancholy, anger, love of death and pessimism are the traits of the Southern Stoic which shaped the vision and mood of the father in terms of which he attempted to kill his son and ultimately committed suicide.

In his consistent efforts to know about the past, Will Barrett comes to know the secret of his father, i.e. death. Like Hamlet, he calls the father "Old mole" telling him that "it was death you loved most of all and loved so surely that wanted to share the secret with me because you loved me too" (p. 126). The father leaves his son, Will Barrett, a terrible legacy; he passes on to his son his fear of life, his fascination with death, legacy of anger and self-loathing. That Will Barrett shares the personality traits of his father is clearly revealed in his father's dialogue with the son on the hunting trip. The father says, "You are like me. We are two of a kind" separate from "The ignorant armies that clash by night" (p. 55). Will Barrett retains the father's anger in his nature which Allison Huger first points out and even he himself sees it. In their confrontation, Will Barrett to collect the balls and Allison to bring them, she asks him, "Are you still climbing on your anger?" (p. 76). Anger repressed is the principal emotion in Will Barrett's life, as it had been in his father's. This repressed anger releases itself at his daughter's marriage rehearsal party when he calls Yamaiuchi, Marion's servant, but he does not turn around. The anger rises in his throat "exactly the same sudden rage his father had turned on the black guide" (p. 171), Will Barrett remembers. Having shared some of the personality traits of his father and knowing that his father was obsessed with death, Will Barrett wonders whether the same obsession will claim his own life.

As the memories of the past crowd Will Barrett's consciousness, the father's voice haunts him. There are a number of long passages of Will Barrett's mental colloquies with the father in which the father insists the son to join him in death. The voice of the father tells the son that he has to make a choice: whether to live in a rotten world or have a courage and integrity to end his life. The father believed that at some time, his son would conclude like his father because suicide is the only solution to the present predicament man forced to live in. The doom of the father hovers over Will Barrett and he seems to yield to it when he tells the father, "You win" (p. 176) meaning that he will follow the example of the father. He combines a suicide plot with an apocalyptic experiment; he descends into Lost Cove cave "looking for proof of the existence of God and a sign of the apocalypse" (p. 198). If no sign of God's existence forthcomes, Will Barrett will by starvation join his father. However, he thinks that his suicide in the cave will represent progress in history of suicide because it is, unlike his father, "done in good faith" (p. 211). He knows that the father's suicide is "wasted" for it proved nothing, solve nothing. Even in the cave the memories of the past chase Will Barrett and the father's voice insists to go ahead. When Will Barrett asks the father what he is doing down here under the earth with him, the father replies, "Because there is no other place for you" (p. 215). Will Barrett's experiment in the cave fails since toothache compels him to leave the place. He comes out of the cave to fall down into Allison's greenhouse giving the novel a new mode.

With the appearance of Allison Hunnicutt Huger, the book becomes a dialectic, highlighting the theme, of death and life, past and future, father and lover, and ending and beginning. Indeed the novel celebrates victory, in Freudian terms, of eros over thanatos and Will Barrett being pulled between these two emotional poles. Allison provides an alternative of eros to thanatos that the father represents. The first encounter between Allison and Will Barrett occurs when she brings the two golf balls and he goes to collect them. He is surprised by Allison holding the balls in two outstretched hands and asking "Are these yours?" (p. 74). There is a symbolic invitation for Will Barrett from Allison to consider her as his love. Allison Huger is in the early twenties, talented and, according to her doctor, psychotic. She has just escaped from the Valleyhead Sanitarious where she had been put as a patient. Her present condition springs from her past which she cannot remember. In the past, Allison has suffered a lot at the hands of her parents. In a sense, they violated her and their violation involves not distance from, but control over their daughter. Kitty and Walter Huber have had high expectation for their daughter, but she short-circuited the parental aspirations. Allison tells, "My mother refused to let me fail. So I insisted" (p. 94). So severe is their manipulative domination that Allison feels continually in danger. She looks for a place to hide herself and first place she seeks is drugs and then the psychosis itself. Allison senses that her problems arise from an inordinate desire to please other people.

But Kitty's story about Allison's conditions differs from what actually happened to her daughter. Kitty tells Will Barrett how Allison remembers her another life, after having one session with Ray, a true mystic, because "her Karma" is too much strong. In her trance Allison saw that she had been a camp follower of the Union Army before the battle of Chancellorsville. She called herself "original hooker", the word first applied to camp followers of General Hooker's army. But Ray in his trance saw Allison as a courtesan spy for the North in Richmond. There she was known as a great Southern belle who charmed many officers with her wit and conversation. To Kitty, these two versions of Allison's another life might be right because there had been a famous Union spy in Richmond who had been a prostitute, a hooker. Kitty thinks that Allison's past of another life explains her present life: in her another life, she knew many men, talked too much, lied too much and abused her body; in this life she knows nobody, never lies, doesn't use her body at all. In such condition Allison has sought a resort of psychosis for that she is subjected to electroshock therapy which has left her with almost no memory. As a result, she has to rely on her "Instructions From Myself To Myself" (p. 27) written before the most recent shock treatment to organize her present life in the greenhouse. Allison's writings in the notebook not only do they guide what to do at the present but also they, what Tremonte calls, "provide her with a history".[15]

After consideration of the character of Allison Huger and Will Barrett, we surmise that they are complementary figures: one supplies what the other lacks and *vice versa*. Percy deliberately intends them to be complementary to each other. The third part of the novel relating to Will Barrett ends with, "He remembered everything" (p. 79) and the fourth part relating to Allison begins with "She remembered nothing" (p. 80). Will Barrett always falls down, Allison hoists the things up so that she assures him, "When you fall down, I'll pick you up" (p. 256). Allison begins her life with learning about the word "love"; Will Barrett struggles with his life by pondering over various names of "death". She mints a fresh language, he can interpret it. These two characters though come together, do not think to let the other know of their respective pasts. Will Barrett never tells Allison about his preoccupation with his past, with suicide, or with God. Neither does Allison tell him about her conflict with her parents or about her experience in the mental hospital. These two fight in their consciousness with their pasts but they still know little of what is going on in each other's mind. Percy's treatment of growing relationship between Allison and Will Barrett owes to a great to his interest in existentialist philosophy. Percy devotes to, considerably, developing intersubjective relationship between the two characters.

While the relationship between Allison and Will Barrett marches on its way to maturity, the past still makes its intrusion on Will Barrett's consciousness. After his physical recovery from harm he received when he fell down the cave, he leaves Allison's greenhouse making his way to his Mercedes. There in his car he suffers from a flashback this time to a trip in the summer after the hunting accident. He and his father had travelled together, to the West Coast as his father attempted to become "pals". Now he realizes that even at the age of thirteen, he knew that since his father could not defeat him by killing him, nothing could or can. "If you didn't defeat me, old mole", Will Barrett says, "loving father and death-dealer, nothing can, not wars, not this century, not the Germans" (p. 270). Yet there is no absolute solution to his problem; if death is in the genes, in the heredity passed to him from his father and grandfather, then his struggle with enemy may not be successful. But a breakthrough is made and he knows the name of enemy—death, and its various names. Knowing the various names of death, Will Barrett will not submit to death because "To know the many names of death is also to know there is life. I choose life" (p. 274). He accuses his father of giving into death. Naming death even grants power over the "death genes" that he fears he may have inherited from his father.

In spite that Will Barrett has acquired knowledge about death, there is no loosening of strong hold of the past on his mind. He still must struggle with "death genes"—that taint in his blood which seems to lead the men in his family to suicide. In one of his spells, he drives his Mercedes up a tree cracking his head on the windshield. Leaving the car there, he wanders to a bus station where he falls into a conversation with a man travelling to Georgia. It is the same place where his father had made his first suicide attempt so Will Barrett has to go there to make 'repetition' or 'return'. In the bus to Georgia, Will Barrett struggles to choose among death and life, past and future. He is not sure whether it is his life that he had left in the Georgia swamps, or death which he had escaped there. Only returning to the scene can tell him but the memory of Allison calls him back. Now his going to Georgia mean "He was losing something. Something of his as solid and heavy and sweet as a pot of honey in his lap was being taken away" (p. 297). Though the physical return to childhood place never occurs in this novel as does in its predecessors, Will Barrett returns to the place in his memory.

Towards the end of the novel, Will Barrett confronts the past finally in order to relieve it. As he approaches the greenhouse, he symbolically kicks down the half-rotten fence that had set off memory of his father's suicide, thus preparing himself for final confrontation with his past. He takes Allison to the Holiday Inn in order to save her from her mother and sheriff who are due to come to take her. Leaving Allison in the inn, Will Barrett goes to consult with his trusted friend about Allison's legal competence. He admits to defend her legal competence in the court. On returning to the Holiday Inn, Will Barrett climbs into bed with Allison who is soundly sleeping. He cannot sleep because he is visited by his father who tempts him to suicide with increasingly most inviting arguments. The father implores Will Barrett "Come, it's the only way, the one quick sure exit of grace and violence and beauty" (pp. 336-37). When Will Barrett persists in saying "No" to his allurements for suicide, the father tells the son that you will do it "because you've got my genes and you know better" (p. 337). Thereupon Will Barrett says "Yes", and then father asks him to go to his car, get the shotgun and kill himself. The son obeys the father, he rises, goes to the Mercedes, takes the shotgun and Luger and walks carrying them to the edge of the gorge. Standing there, in a surprised move, he flings the guns into space and turns to go back to Allison, not even waiting for them to hit bottom. Minutes later, the lovers finally make love for the first time, and Ero's victory over Thanatos is complete. At the close of *The Second Coming*, Will Barrett is exorcised the past relating to his father's suicide by allowing the memory to return and then confronting it to put it aside.

Following its predecessors, Percy's last novel *The Thanatos Syndrome** (1987) describes the theme of the past and the Southern character in its own way. The novel reintroduces Dr. Tom More as a narrator-protagonist, however changed to a certain degree and his reappearance makes the novel sequel to *Love in the Ruins*. As a changed character, Tom More is not an alcoholic but an older and wiser Southerner in his fifties having acute sense of past with concurrent sense of ending. The Southerners' sense of ending or, their sense of death or, their sense of apocalypse claims its root in the defeat in the Civil War which affected the religious pattern in the South adding to it the element of apocalypse. More importantly, the Southerner's response to the 'modern mind', which is the embodiment of the change followed the Civil War, accompanies terror. They see in modern mind what Cash calls "the Faustian hell-compact, a gigantic conspiracy to crush truth out of the world, loose the beast in man, and strip them of their ancient sway".[16] Tom More's view of the modern mind is not different from what Cash describes; he sees Dr. Bob Comeaux and Van Dorn as modern *avtar* of Faust who are engaged in a conspiracy against society. As a doctor, gentleman of "Feliciana" country—a distinctive region—Tom More discharges his duty to his patients up to the level of a doctor and a gentleman. He knows how to act in a given situation that is the foremost trait of a gentleman. Bob Comeaux appreciates this trait of Tom More saying that "You're the proper Southern gent who knows how to act", and adds "You have style" (p. 347). When Tom More senses the conspiracy of

---

* Walker Percy, *The Thanatos Syndrome* (New York: Farrar Straus and Giroux, 1987). All subsequent references in the text are to this edition.

Bob Comeaux and Van Dorn against the people, he sets out to save the people at any cost he will have to pay.

The novel opens with the protagonist noticing "something strange is occurring in our region" (p. 3) just after he is released from prison where he served time for selling drugs to truck drivers. During his two years stay in prison, Tom More learns about the present age including many other things. What he learns of the present age is, in a sense, his diagnosis of the present civilization based on his study of history. His reading a new history of the Battle of Somme enables him to conclude that the two battles, the Battle of Somme and the Battle of Verdun, are "events marking the beginning of a new age" which might be described as the "the age of thanatos" (p. 87). Tom More's obsession with the Stedman history evokes in him the sense of ending which lasts throughout the novel. This is clearly stated towards the end of the novel when he goes on a trip to the Disney World with his wife and children. There he reads Stedman in the car when he comes out in the delightful people, he reacts "I experience the sensation that the world really ended in 1916 and that we've been living in a dream ever since" (p. 339). With the new knowledge that he has acquired in the prison, Tom More can see symptoms producing death in society that Percy calls the thanatos syndrome. What else Tom More learns in the prison is "a certain detachment" and a "low-grade curiosity" which in fact not only enables him "to notice small things" around but also to carry out a search leading to the cause of the things (p. 67). The small things Tom More notices are related to his patients in whom he sees certain personality changes. His old patients who earlier suffered from depression, anxiety, phobias, now display "a curious flatness of tone" (p. 68) or, as he says at one point, "They've all turned into chickens" (p. 90). No more high exaltations and morning terror for them. Even in his wife Ellen, Tom More sees a definite change. She had become materialistic, acquisitive, hard drinking and more competitive at bridge. His other women patients show changes in their sexual habits presenting and exhibiting other signs of estrus behavior. Considering all these changes in the patients, Tom More asks "Is this a syndrome? If so, what is its etiology?" The syndrome that Tom More mentions here is the thanatos syndrome and he attempts to find out its cause.

Fired by curiosity and concern for the patients, Tom More undertakes a search to track the mystery of the thing. The search includes his horizontal as well as vertical journey to different places exploring and exposing, satirically, modern man's dream of perfection. As a detective in a mystery tale, Tom More searches the truth slowly as he solves the puzzle piece by piece. The search is marked by Tom More's intense individualism, a trait of Southern behavior, because though he seeks help from Dr. Lucy Lipscomb and other, he never speaks about it to her, or anyone in the novel. His search is more personal so heroic; he is purely self-asserting from the beginning to the end in the search. Above all, having the sense of the past and the sense of ending, Tom More carries out the search more successfully. Tom More's first visit to Father Rinaldo Smith in the tower—a vertical journey—reminds him of his search and makes him known of the situation down in society. In their meeting, Father Smith tells Tom More that he can no longer preach because the words do not signify; they are deprived of their meaning. He has gone to the top of tower because he is angry at the people below for living in wickedness, falling away from faith and into the hands of Satan who is waiting for the final war to send him millions of souls. Father Smith mistakes Tom More for a member of doctors to turn their backs on the back of Hippocrates and kill millions of useless people, unborn children, born malformed children "for the good of mankind" (p. 127). Father Smith's comment is not so much directed at Tom More as at Bob Comeaux and Van Dorn. Before Tom More leaves the tower, Father Smith tells him "I think you're on to something extremely important", and at the same time warns him "There are dangers down there, Tom, you may not be aware of" (p. 131). But Tom More has sensed something similar to that Father Smith wants to tell him and in order to define it, he has undertaken a search.

Tom More's visit to the plantation Pantherburn—a horizontal journey—owned by his cousin Dr. Lucy Lipscomb turns out as his visit to the world of the past. On the way to Lucy, the green and pleasant geography reminds Tom More of the past of the rich English planters who painted the birds and taught dancing for living. Back toward the river and Grand Mer, there is a great widening of the river into a gulf where the English landed with their slaves from the Indies, took up indigo farming, and lived the happy life of Feliciana. Tom More's memory of the past is not nostalgic but the life wish of the old people, he thinks, is worth to appreciate in a world governed by death wish. There stands semblance of the old world, Lucy's plantation Pantherburn with its two thousand acres; its façade, gallery and public rooms for living and dining are decorated in the old style with heavy silverware and worn oriental rugs. Then there is uncle Hugh Bob with his memories of the past and of the Second World War. He tells Tom More how the Yankees stole everything in the house except the silver inset handles and how General Van Dorn slept in Dupre's room in Pantherburn overnight. He cherishes the memory of his experience in World War Second in Germany where he lived with a German girl for three weeks. Uncle's memory of the war and the German girl prepares a way for Tom More's later comment on how romanticism made the Southerners to view war as romantic adventure.

Tom More's encounter with Lucy brings forth much of his mind. He sees Lucy as a reminder of the past, of the Southern women in old novels—a splendid girl, not beautiful but full of teasing and high spirits. To him she is a Southern Belle, the traditional model of feminine behavior in the old South, in a white-columned mansion. He tells, "She reminds me of a chatelaine, the ole, miss of Pantherburn" (p. 146). Her sight and her smell evoke the by-gone days in the form of déjà vu in Tom More's consciousness. The form of déjà vu, which overtakes him in company of Lucy has to do with, he tells, cars, women, girls, youth, the past and the old U.S.A. Though Lucy retains much of the Old South, she does not avert the idea of the New South. The plantation Pantherburn is decorated in the old style but back in the private windowless room, Lucy has well lighted lab stocked with computers. And only here with the help of Lucy and her computer, Tom More makes a real breakthrough in his search. He and Lucy conclude that the patients may have heavy sodium (Na-24) poisoning because the poisoning pattern in Feliciana follows the water supply. Van Dorn's Grand Mer nuclear power plant had heavy sodium reactor and it is less than a mile from water intake. Tom More hypothesizes that the reactor is being leaked into the water or, as Lucy says, being added deliberately to the water. The effect of the heavy sodium on the patients is very frightening; there is decrease of human symptoms such as anxiety, depression, stress, insomnia, suicidal tendencies and chemical dependence. Essentially these characters have become more normal psychologically, but less human as Tom More tells Lucy, "Think of it as a regression from a stressful human existence to a peaceful animal existence" (p. 180). Although heavy sodium seems to create some positive, attractive results, it ultimately produces a kind of death—a death of human spirit.

Being a gentleman and knowing how to act, Tom More sets out to see the Ratliff intake in order to be certain about it. His journey from the plantation Pantherburn to Grand Mer with Virgil Bon and Uncle Hugh Bob in a boat is yet another occasion for Tom More to review the Southern past. As their boat passes over the water of Lake Mary, Tom More tells that this clear stretch of water once was a Grand Mer where the boats were loaded with cotton and indigo and unloaded with grand piano, port wine, even one or two books of Shakespeare, John Bunyan and later Sir Walter Scott by the hundreds. He adds how Walter Scott was "as inevitable as the King James Bible" in every plantation house and the same "Walter Scott sending all these English-Americans to war against the Yankees as if they were the Catholic nights in *Ivanhoe* gone off to fight the infidel" (p. 181). What Percy wants to emphasize here is the fact that the Southerner's craving for death in the form of their willingness to fight is a direct result of the imported romanticism of Scott.

Tom More's interview, a part of his search, with Bob Comeaux after Tom's release from the jail where he was temporarily held, is significant because it reveals that the addition of heavy sodium to water is a means to fulfill Comeaux's dreams of ideal society, and also his rationalization of that dream as the restoration of the Southern past. Dr. Bob Comeaux, the modern Faust tells Tom More that dosing the people with the heavy sodium produces tremendous results in the society as if he waves a magic wand and change the society overnight. "What would you say if I gave you magic wand you could wave over there...and overnight you could reduce crime in the streets by eighty-five percent?" (p. 191), Comeaux asks. An experimental project Blue Boy—a magic wand—headed by Bob Comeaux is aimed at eradicating social problem and Comeaux comes out with its results. Since the start of the project the child abuse has been reduced by eighty-seven per cent, hospital admission for depression, chemical dependence and anxiety by seventy-nine per cent. The heavy sodium does affect the female biology effecting the regression from menstrual cycle to estrus. While the female human is in heat seventy-five per cent of the time, the percentage falls to nine percent for the female mammal. Not only is this "a marvellous built-in natural population control" (p. 196) but more significantly it means the end of useless sex, as modern Faust describes it, "goodbye pills, rubbers, your friendly abortionist. Goodbye promiscuity, goodbye sex" (p. 197). Thus Bob Comeaux's Blue Boy project aims at "improving the quality of life for the individual" (p. 190), and seeks solutions to all problems through technology.

What we learn from Bob Comeaux is his concern for "the decay of the social fabric" (p. 265). His dream is social, sometimes cultural and even sectional too. To him the ideal society is the society of the Old South in which people knew their way of life. In a sense, his dream is regressive, looking backward rather than forward. That Comeaux's dream has to do with the restoration of the Southern mythical past is obvious in his talk with Tom More. "Tom, would you laugh at me if I told you what we've done is restore the best of the Southern Way of Life? Would think that too corny?" (p. 197),

Comeaux asks. In his attempt to restore the elegance and graciousness of the Southern way of life, Bob Comeaux admits stratified society in which every stratum is separated. In this context, the social disruption is the evil, the plague that threatens the order of society. For the social disruption Bob Comeaux holds the blacks responsible as it is recognizable in his use of stereotypical image, such as "young Punks", "rape your daughter" (pp. 197-198). The Southerners have developed a rape complex which implies there is a subconscious fear that the white woman will be raped by the black. The restoration of the old order of society of the South clearly means that the blacks and the white thrash must return to their stratum where they were belonged. Bob Comeaux's dream makes safe return of the blacks if not to their African origins but to the practice of their native art. Thus restricting the blacks to their native art, Bob will have an orderly society that he dreams of.

The nature of Bob Comeaux's dream of restoring the best of the Southern way of life is again revealed in his remarks to Tom More who is temporarily back in prison. Comeaux says, "There is still grace, style, beauty, manners, civility left in the world. It's not all gone with the wind" (p. 265). Here the words grace, style, etc. are the best of the Southern way of life and the reference to Margaret Mitchell's *Gone with the Wind* echoes Ashley's yearning for a motionless society. What Bob Comeaux wants to suggest to Tom More is that if the disruptive elements be controlled and immobilized, then the antebellum society could be restored in the present. Bob Comeaux has his dream of an orderly society sanctioned even by Jefferson, as it is clear here, "We're not talking about 'old massa' and his niggers. We're not talking about Uncle Tom. We're talking about Uncle Tom Jefferson and his yeoman farmer and yeoman craftsman" (p. 198). Here, Bob Comeaux modifies the view of Jefferson who never made the black the yeoman craftsman. But he does not bother about the facts. Instead he refers to Jefferson what he thought Jefferson was. The sole purpose of Comeaux is that his dream must be sanctioned by actual history and thereby to make Tom More to join the Blue Boy project. He asks Tom More to help him to stop the ongoing "decay of the social fabric" (p. 265). However, Tom More sees Comeaux's dream of restoration of the mythical past as a sham since the Blue Boy project effects the symbolic death of human race and he would flout his appeal. Tom More finds that the language of the patients is diminished and with it diminished their being. The consciousness which is the locus of the past, is damned by Comeaux as "the scourge and curse of life on this earth" (p. 195). Tom More fears the danger of breaking the life of the people loose from its past moorings.

The Blue Boy project of Comeaux also encompasses a component of real, physical death. By accepting euthanasia (literally "easy death") of the terminally ill, they might to easily move to euthanasia of abused infants and unwanted elderly. Here the scientists' aim of improving quality of life harks back to the Nazi dream of perfection that Father Smith warns Tom More in the tower. In his confession, Father Rinaldo Smith tells Tom More about his meeting the most prominent psychiatrists and eugenicists of the Weimer Republic in Germany. Then he never thought that these cultivated, scholarly men who in few years, would preside over the murders of countless numbers of the unfit in Hitler's hospital and death camps. During his tale of his experience in Germany, Father Smith asks Tom More "Do you think we're different from the Germans?" (p. 256). With this question, Father Smith wants to communicate a message that the attempts of the scientists, whether they are Germans or Americans, to better society will inevitably end up with killing the innocents.

Father Smith carries the burden of the past related to his experience in Germany. While in Germany, Rinaldo was impressed by Fascism because "Fascism was then thought of as a bundle of sticks, faces, stronger than one stick and not necessarily a bad thing" (p. 241), Father Smith tells. As Rinaldo's interest grew in Nazi ideal, he felt admiration for his cousin Helmut who joined the Nazi force. Father Smith admits that if he had been German and not American, he would have joined Helmut. This is the burden Father Smith carries until he confesses it to Tom More. For his fascination to the Nazi ideal, Father Smith holds his own father responsible; his father's self-indulgent romanticism led him to idolize the iron-willed young Nazi Helmut Jager. Father Smith tells that his father was "a type familiar in the South, not successful in life but an upholder of culture, lofty ideals, and the higher things" (p. 241). Being a romantic, his father was a music lover and when in Germany, he was invited to join the chamber-music group of Dr. Jager and his friend. They played Brahms, while his father at piano tears in his eyes. Fascination with Germany has a part of the Southerners consciousness. Father Smith makes it clear when he says "being a student at Heidelberg was as much a part of the Southern tradition as reading Sir Walter Scott" (p. 240). Fascination with the Germans led the Southerners to imitate them as it is proved in Father Smith's case and in Comeaux's Blue Boy project.

Father Smith's association of the scientist's ideal of improving upon the society with Hitler's gas chamber parallels with what Tom more thinks of the Blue Boy project. Exploring the mystery, Tom More comes upon the fact that John Van Dorn assists Comeaux in his social engineering by supplying the heavy sodium. If Dr. Comeaux is a modern Faust, then Van Dorn is his modern servant, Wagner assisting his master. According to the local paper, Van Dorn is a Renaissance man; computer wizard, world-class contract bridge player, headmaster of an exclusive school. He claims to have been a Southerner in the neighboring state of Mississippi, but Tom More sees there is something a bit stagy about his manner and speech. On a fishing trip when Van Dorn tells Tom More that he is back to his "own people" and a "way of life" (p. 59) thereupon Tom More reacts "If there is such a thing as a Southern way of life, part of it has to do with not speaking of it" (p. 60). The fishing trip provides Tom More with an occasion to judge and deflate Van Dorn's Southernism. Van Dorn recently bought the plantation house, Belle Ame, named from the French "beautiful soul", and it is restored to its antebellum splendor. The physical plant at Belle Ame is beautiful and so typical of everyone's image of a Southern plantation that has been used as a set for several movies. Now Belle Ame is used to run a public school founded "to revive the traditional Southern academy founded on Greek ideals of virtue" (p. 214). But in reality, behind its façade, the school children are molested sexually by making them drink the contaminated water. The plantation house, Belle Ame provides contrast to the plantation house, Pantherburn; one is fake, the other is genuine.

The master of the plantation school, Van Dorn, instead of teaching the Greek ideals of virtue, advocates the sexual liberation of civilization and that is the ultimate goal. His heroes are Einstein with his repressed Jewish sexuality and Don Juan with his sexual frivolity. He claims to have gotten to the origins of love and affection by initiating young children into sex. Van Dorn is more villainous than Comeaux. Tom More and Lucy discover that the children in the school are not only being given the treated water, but also been sexually abused. They also discover the child pornography that Van Dorn and his curious band of associates have produced. Tom More learns that the school children at Belle Ame outperform themselves physically and intellectually but lost spiritually. Once the syndrome is defined, Tom More can see the danger looming over the young children as well as over the society, both need to be helped. He knows the dangerous consequences of the social engineering, which is nothing but a conspiracy against society. He prepares to raid the Belle Ame with the help of Virgil and Uncle in order to seek the final evidence of Van Dorn's worst proclivities to foil his scheme. At Belle Ame, Tom More as a good cowboy, forces Van Dorn and his company to drink the modal sodium. What follows is the funniest episode in the novel in which the tutors revert to ape behavior, going about on all fours, picking lice and grooming one another. Creating a concrete evidence of proclivities, Tom More successfully routs out the secret scheme of Bob Comeaux and Van Dorn.

NOTES

1. Lewis A. Lawson, *Following Percy: Essays on Walker Percy's Work* (New York: The Whitson Pub. Co., 1988), p. 76.
2. Max Webb, "Binx Bolling's New Orleans: Moviegoer, Southern Writing, and Father Abraham", *The Art of Walker*

Percy: Stratagems for Being, ed. Panthea Reid Broughton (Baton Rouge & London: Louisana State UP., 1979), p. 5.

3. Janet Hobbs, "Binx Bolling and the Stages on Life's Way", *The Art of Walker Percy: Stratagem for Being,* p. 37.
4. William Rodney Allen, *Walker Percy: A Southern Wayfarer* (Jackson & London: UP. of Mississippi, 1986), p. 31.
5. Allen, p. 35.
6. Linda W. Hobson, *Understanding Walker Percy* (South Carolina: Univ. of S. Carolina Press, 1988), p. 52.
7. Lewis A. Lawson, "Walker Percy's Southern Stoic", *Southern Literary Journal,* III-I (Fall, 1970), p. 21.
8. Martin Luschei, *The Sovereign Wayfarer: Walker Percy's Diagnosis of the Malaise* (Baton Rouge: Louisiana State UP., 1992), p. 155.
9. Allen, p. 71.
10. Mary Deems Howland, *The Gift of Other: Gabriel Marcel's Concept of Intersubjectivity in Walker Percy's Novel* (Pittsburg, Pennsylvania: Duguesne UP., 1990), p. 60.
11. W.B. Yeats, "The Second Coming", *W.B. Yeats: Selected Poetry,* ed. Timothy Webb (London: Clays Ltd. St. Ives Plc., 1991), p. 124.
12. William Leigh Godshalk, "Love in the Ruins: Thomas More's Distorted Vision", *The Art of Walker Percy: Stratagem for Being,* p. 142.
13. Lewis A. Lawson, *Following Percy: Essays on Walker Percy's Work* (Troy, New York: The Whitson Publishing Company, 1988) p. 157.
14. Mary K. Sweeny, *Walker Percy and the Postmodern World* (3441 North Ashland Avenue Chicago: Loyola UP., 1987), p. 23.
15. Colleen M. Tremonte, "The Poet-prophet and Feminine Capability in Walker Percy's *The Second Coming",* *Mississippi Quarterly,* XLIII-2 (Spring, 1990), p. 176.
16. W.J. Cash, *The Mind of the South* (New York: Alfred A. Knopf, 1968), p. 138.

3

Shelby Foote

*Tournament** (1949) the first novel by Shelby Foote originally written in his early twenties, reveals the young writer's intense preoccupation with history as is seen in his treatment of his central character, Hugh Bart. Presenting the character of Bart, Foote shows how Bart's preoccupation with past, in the form of pattern and style, becomes an enclosure for him barring him from the present and future. The action of the novel, though primarily concerned with the rise and fall of Bart, is governed by his obsession with the past. The novel is set in a period after the Reconstruction when the people of the South are building up social and economic order out of social and economic chaos. Bart launches his career in such a significant transitional period in Southern history. Owing to the region's code of chivalry which demands decisive action in the times of crisis, Bart fights to rebuild the Solitaire and shape his life into the old ways destroyed by the Northern invaders. Life for Bart, as suggested by the title, is a "tournament"—a number of competitions of skills in each the game is played by the long—established rules. And a "tournament", is what Phillips, Jr. says "a useful substitute for war, a crucible from which heroes emerge".[1] He is fit for "tournament" because he is, as the narrator, Asa describes, "a man cast in the heroic mold" (p. xxx), a necessary quality for the player.

---

* Shelby Foote, *Tournament* 2nd ed. (Birmingham, Alabama: Summa Publications, 1987). All subsequent references in the text are to this edition.

As the novel opens, Bart has just begun his four-year term as a sheriff of Issawamba County that marks the beginning of his rise. He is elected in because he has an ability at hunting, a game, and has "some inner hand for making the small farmers and tradesmen admire the way he sat a horse and picked a crop" (p. xxx). Even his principal opponent in the election, Judge Wiltner, soon becomes his admirer so when the Insurance Company asks his advice about Solitaire, a large bankrupt plantation, the judge recommends Bart's name. Bart proves the judge's belief in his capacity true and buys the plantation Solitaire to replace it with its past glory. The history of the plantation Solitaire is the history of the South: Issac Jameson, the first settler, carved the plantation out of wilderness; his son Clive Jameson built the Solitaire and lived there to see the cotton empire and the house being destroyed by the Northern invaders. Defeat in the war made Jameson to mortgage the plantation to procure money necessary to "start again" and it remained unpaid until it is foreclosed. Now Bart has the charge of one of the largest plantations—five square miles of the richest farmland and a forty-room mansion stood on it. In describing the story of the Solitaire, Foote reviews Southern history from the early settlers first arrived to the time when the region was drawn into the devastating war.

Bart's move to farm the plantation and acquire its attendant grand style is his attempt to establish himself in the traditional role of a planter. He creates the cotton kingdom for "he planted almost nothing but cotton" (p. 15). Since farming to him is a game played according to the rules, his early years are marked by fierce activities on the farm. He rises before dawn and gets maximum of work out of field hands. To oversee the work on the plantation, Bart keeps an overseer with whom he holds three conferences during a day. In spite of the odds sets by nature, success comes to Bart, makes him able to pay off the mortgage within ten years and six months. After clearing the mortgage, Bart has established himself in his role as a planter and the game seems to be won. He becomes a wealthy planter, "biblical in the rich", Billy Boy, his long-time servant thinks of him (p. xxix). The Solitaire has its new glare, its windows wear their velvet; the bed is polished and made; new furniture is installed. Now Bart can afford entertainment and a sense of noblesse oblige-characteristics of a planter.

Bart engages himself in other games such as hunting, shooting and cards, which are the sources of relief and entertainment for planter. On hunting, he gets "pleasure out of the hard recoil of the gun, the acrid smell of powder blown back across his face" (p. 35). In the game of hunting, he becomes champion setting the ducks-bagged record which is not broken. During cold weather the planters play poker in a hunting lodge, which they built at the upper end of the Jordan Lake for the purpose. For one month he has watched the game and once he has learned the essentials of it, he starts to play. When hunting becomes lesser in the Delta, it gives way to trapshooting. The Ithaca Gun Club holds contests in which the main contestant is Bart who wins the tri-state competition in Memphis. Finally, he wins the national trapshooting championship that gives him the opportunity to shake hands with President Taft. These games, no doubt, greatly help Bart to enter into the planters' circle and observe their grand style in order to imbibe it.

Soon as Bart moves to the Solitaire, he begins to acquire the region's grand style that he conceives of as "composed not so much of the large actions and possessions but rather of the small, undisguised and apparently birth-acquired habits and gestures" (p. 18). Though he has not come to Jordan County with any preconception about the region's grand style, it is not difficult for him to find it there. He watches those around him and begins to imitate them. Asa, the narrator describes that he "watched, and as he watched he began to acquire; from this man he took one things from that another" (p. 18). Bart is very much careful in moving his hands and pushing his hat and talking to others in order to preserve his "air of gentility" (p. 19). He thinks that men admire him for his new garment and acquired gestures so he becomes proud. He can't think that people like not for his garment but for "the glimpses of what the garments was meant to cover" (p. 19). His preoccupation with the traditional manners is so strong that the moment he realizes he has dropped his air of gentility, "he would snap shut like a turtle jerking back into its carapace" (p. 19). Thus the past in the form of traditional manners becomes for Bart a shell that encloses him.

In his attempt to fit himself in the old style of the planter, Bart realizes that wife and family are important next to the gestures. He carefully observes the planters' families around so that he "knew perfectly what it was he wanted to duplicate" (p. 22). He celebrates the Christmas Day in 1888 among various planters, families on the lake and he comes to know what he wants to become a planter. He needs a wife, so he marries Florence Jameson whom he never considers as a companion of love but the keeper of the Solitaire and the mother of his heirs. After the marriage, Bart thinks he has a "bride" but "the word meant nothing, brought no image" until he changes the word into "wife" (p. 23). Now the word "wife" brings to him an image of a woman like those others he has seen around carrying the keys at their belt. To Bart, Florence is a "chatelaine" of the Solitaire, the keeper of the keys like other women who call their husbands "Mister" all their lives. To Bart who is born and brought up in another country, marriage is "the seal set on his invasion of the planter kingdom" (p. 36).

After having wife, Bart raises the family because the pattern of life of the planter requires heirs who will be reared according to "the strict formula whereby life was simple" (p. 36). In keeping with the "formula" the boys are sent to "military preparatory schools then either to Ole Miss of Sewanee" (p. 92). In these schools "they wore brass buttons and learned the manual of arms along with a smattering of history" (p. 93). Then, after this preliminary education, if they choose a profession such as medicine, or law, or the army, they go to an Eastern university, Harvard or Virginia. But the real education of the Delta young begins when they return to the plantation and learn from their father's overseer how to farm cotton. The intention behind training the young boys on the farms is, Asa says, "the repetition of a cycle, maintenance of a static life-way" (p. 92). Hunting and poker and drinking are the pastime for them, and above this, it is the accepted belief that "the way to test a gentleman was to take him hunting, play high-stake cards with him, or get him drunk" (p. 93). Their initiation into sex is either with a "sullen Negro girl" or a "boisterous Negro prostitute" because "the code...made white girls untouchable" (p. 93). The girls, too, are raised by the pattern existing there for the white female. They follow the roles of their mothers, or in other words, they follow their "female share of the pattern" (p. 95). In fine, their role in the planter society is the chatelaines—the keeper of the plantation house. It is this way of life of young people—male and female—is "the pattern laid out" for Bart's children (p. 95). Bart is keen enough to see his children to follow the pattern.

Bart's children do not follow the established pattern so to Bart they have failed. The older son Hugh who looks like his father is more delicate in features and shyer in manners. He has not done well at the military academy in Tennessee so that the commandant "complained of Hugh's failure to apply himself" (p. 133). The problem with him, as the commandant says, has been indolence which is "a sort of tactical inertia by which he avoided exertion in all its forms" (p. 133). Hugh fails to form an idea about his future even after he has finished at the academy thus contradicting with his father who has worked hard all his life with a goal before him. He is poor not only at the university but also at drinking that is one of the tests a gentleman has to pass. For Bart, a gentleman has to drink on occasion but he should be able to walk home alone. He tells Hugh "If you can't come home standing alone, moving on your own two legs and holding your head up...don't drink" (p. 155). Hugh's early marriage with Kate Bateman ends his career at the university and he turns to farming but within a year he fails there too. He does not want to farm without knowing why and thereafter Bart tells him, "If you don't want Solitaire, I reckon Solitaire don't want you" (p. 178). A week later, Bart arranges to sell the farm for the quarter of a million dollars and moves to town.

Bart's younger son Clive and the daughter Florence are no better; they too have failed in terms of the established pattern. Florence becomes a mystery for Bart because of the way she behaves. At the age of twelve, she becomes "calculatingly disobedient" (p. 123), and at fourteen she behaves like a tomboy fighting the boys behind the barn than receiving them "as caller in the parlor" (p. 132). At the age of seventeen when other girls are romantic, Florence "saved no dance cards, made no scrap book, kept no romantic diary" (p. 158). Instead of following the pattern laid out for the Delta female, Florence turns out to be a lesbian. The letter written by the teachers explaining the reason of Florence's expulsion from Virginia boarding school says that at night "she was going after the other girls under the sheets" (p. 237). By the time Bart receives the letter, he is about to go to Kentucky to defend his trapshooting time, but he gives it up. Clive has been Bart's favorite, but he is spoiled and becomes unpopular among other children. When he is almost fourteen, he falls from the high roof of the rented house in Bristol. He is saved from the accident, but is doomed to wheel chair for the rest of his life. In his delirium Clive sees Bart as chasing him; he tells his mother "I fell off the roof and he laughed. He pushed me" (p. 196). The day on which Clive accuses his father turns out as the day of Memphis Bank's failure that brings Bart's complete ruin.

Bart's move to sell the plantation is caused not so much by his children's failure as his willingness to measure that failure by the pattern of history. When he sees his children have failed in terms of the pattern and are unable to assume the responsibility of their heritage, he sells the plantation, puts his money in the bank and moves to town. In Bart's view the traditional pattern of life is a goal enough for a man to achieve and it is his fault against which Judge Wiltner warns him. Three weeks before his death, the judge calls Bart to his bedside and tells him that he has stopped growing because what are steps along the way, now they have become for Bart "the edifice"—a goal, a destination (p. 52). The judge advises him to come out of the pattern and move to a large goal, "make a good farmer" (p. 52), he tells, otherwise he will die with things crashed in his lap. But the judge's warning does not shake Bart's stance toward the pattern and still he does constrict himself to the superficial style of life in the Delta. The judge who first sees in Bart the "spark" which leads him to success now can see the enclosures around Bart of the barriers and the games through which he will fall.

Bart fails to see the essence of the past that farming gives meaning to pattern and style. Since he misses it, he fails; or rather the past fails him as it fails Clive Jameson, Abe Wisten, Major Dubose and Cassendale Tarfeller whose examples Bart disregards. Tarfeller is "the last male of a line" (p. 39) of the original settlers of the Lake Jordan County who inherits a plantation and the wealth along with it. He takes no interest in farming because "neither the concentration nor the labor required by farming was possible for a person with his temperament" (p. 39). But he adopts the outward form of the Delta planter and he possesses the needed gentility. His clothes are "neat and carefully fitted" and his manners are "perfect" so he becomes a part of the society of the lake planters (p. 39). Tarfeller has a younger daughter Bertha who sees how her father is dominated by her mother and concludes that her father is not a man. She always wants to escape from her father so at first she entertains the thought of suicide then she gives herself to Downs Macready a 'gambler' seeing in him a savior and seducer. Knowing the affairs, Tarfeller's wife asks Tarfeller to challenge the man who has 'defiled' his daughter. Having the romantic view of the past, Tarfeller thinks the dual to be conducted in a manner described by "the elder Dumas or Walter Scott" (p. 44). Since Tarfeller is not fit for the role, for the tournament that both his wife and the traditional code ask him to play, he is easy prey to the gambler. He lays in the dust stained but not bloody because "the dignity of bleeding were denied him in his belated assumption of a heritage for which he had never been fit" (p. 47). It is history that becomes the cause of Tarfeller's death; "The past had brought him to death in the dust" (p. 47), Asa says.

Tarfeller is killed because, like Bart's children, he is not fit for the heritage; Bart is ruined because he allows the games and pattern to enclose him. Bart's preoccupation with the planter style in general prevents him from dealing with his wife and children with love. He is so much preoccupied with it that there is no room for romance or courtship between him and his wife Florence. He sees her twice before he speaks of marriage and after marriage, he plans a week-long honeymoon trip in New Orleans but it lasts only two days. His sex with Florence, since conditioned by the style, becomes an act without feeling. "It would be careful and controlled", Asa tells, "Bart holding his weight on knees and elbows and maintaining an even breath because any display would be distasteful" (p. 84). This pattern of sex is broken down temporarily by Florence after the death of the first Clive. Now she no longer waits for her husband's signal, rolls against him "rigorous, spasmodic, urgent" and makes "little throaty sounds of passion" which makes Bart aghast and leaves him confusing (p. 91). This change lasts until Florence conceives again and has a promise of replacement for the loss of the child. Even this passionless pattern of sex disappears in Bristol to which the family moves after the plantation is sold. There as Bart climbs into bed careful not to touch Florence, waits for sleep to come.

Bart's obsession with the games and the pattern excludes him from his family. At first Bart enjoys spending time with his children when they are young, but as they become older, he no longer speaks to them. His camaraderie though serves him well in his relations with men, becomes a source of his isolation from his children. Bart's engaging himself in trapshoots, in hunting and in poker leaves him with a little time to spend in his family. Asa tells that "Bart had been away from home so much this past year, he hardly knew any of his children" (p. 132). After the sale, Bart moves to Bristol with his family, there, too, he remains away from home; "Poker was everything now" (p. 189), Asa tells. His absences in the family make him an outcast even in his home where he moves "cautiously, like a hostage among enemies, into and out of Mrs. Bart's stolid contemplation, Clive's accusing stare, Florence's disinterest" (p. 213). The fall of Bart is understood only in the context of the Southern history and its attendant Southern character. That the Southerners are fated to fail, is true because the seeds of their fall lie in history, in their defeat in the Civil War. Bart trying to analyze his own past thinks that "each year had prepared for the next, had held the seeds of what followed" (pp. 212-13).

This sense of history makes the Southerner to reconstruct the past so that Bart towards the end of his life is found in a desperate need to recount his personal history. Bart tries to tell it to the peddler, Arthur Sunday but he is not interested to listen to it. To Bart, his past life is a succession of "facts" and omitting them means only describing "a man's appearance by displaying his skeleton" (pp. 212-23). The facts which are individual "bead" are related to all the lives that have touched Bart's and has a share in his telling. He can't omit any of the facts since it would mean "a space left blank on a canvas larger than life" (p. 223). But to tell it properly, Bart thinks, will need as much time as has been required to live it. What he needs is a "link" a hidden "string" to join the facts in order to make a unique story, a whole. The link is there in his house in the person of Asa, his grandson whose features are the same as his grandfather's. Lifting him up, Bart sees into Asa's eyes that are "so much like his own" (p. 224). It is Asa who will link individual facts in Bart's life; he is a living fusion of the past and the present.

*Follow Me Down** (1950), the second novel by Shelby Foote, tells of a Southern farmer who is deeply obsessed with the history of his region, the South and acts accordingly in the present. Once again that Foote's interest is in the history of the South is obvious here but this time the focus is upon a subtler ingredient of Southern past; the conservative religion and its concomitant emotionalism. From the time of the early settlement the South has been a center for Protestant evangelical fundamentalism—the heart of the South's conservative religion—that has emphasized on private morality, anti-fun and highly individualistic moral orientation. The Bible, the Word of God, has provided the Old South with a firm foundation for its religious faith to be built upon. Because of its religious fundamentalism, the Southern society

---

* Shelby Foote, *Follow Me Down* (New York, Random House, 1978). All subsequent references in the text are to this edition.

has remained comparatively static till the Reconstruction unleashes the forces of change. Filled with the fear of change, the South in its mood of defense gives way to the savage ideal of religion. Jehovah, the God of the Old Testament, becomes a tribal God—a god of punishment—and the scripture is quoted to support causes and a warning is sounded against the modern Jezebels, the wicked women. In the face of change, the Southern mind is deeply obsessed with the past religion and Luther Dade Eustis embodies that obsessed mind in the novel.

Eustis, the protagonist and one of the narrators, is presented as the Southerner dominated by the past of the region. It is so because he was brought up under the formative influences of history. As a boy who lost his parents, he lives with his grandfather, the Civil War Veteran. Since he has lost his parents the only key person in his life is his grandfather whose influence on Eustis is easily visible. "Anyone with him five minutes could see", Eustis's wife tells, "that the main person in his life was the grandfather, the one-armed veteran with the tales of war, of the battle where he'd been hurt and seen General Johnston die from a wounded leg" (pp. 200-201). The influence of this grandfather is so much on Eustis as he wants to sustain the chivalric tradition of the family. He wished to be drafted in the army but fails because he was too young for that. However, his obsession with the family's chivalric past continues and he desires to have a male child that can sustain the tradition of the warriors. All men in the South want a son but with Eustis, his wife tells, "it was something special" (p. 207). Failed to have a male child, he turns to religion. He is inspired by Brother Jimson's sermon on Original Sin and Redemption. He becomes a highly religious man dominated by a desire to follow the letter of the Holy Bible. Chivalric aspect of Southern history is replaced by the fundamental one in Eustis's case.

Foote emphasizes upon Eustis's fundamentalism by making him the inhabitant of the Solitaire which, for Foote, is the symbol of the traditional Southern society of orthodox nature. And Eustis's association with the flocks preached by Brother Jimson, the old fashioned preacher believing the savage ideal of religion, further underlines the fundamentalism of Eustis. The preacher is the man who punished a young sinner by dashing him against a tree with a physical strength thus displaying the nature of his religion. He has become the preacher by attending not any seminary but he tells, "On word from the Lord" (p. 248). There is no way for Eustis to escape the influence of Brother Jimson. What follows in Eustis's life after he meets Beulah Ross must be seen in the light of his obsession with the fundamental religion. The encounter between Eustis and Beulah is a crucial event in the novel because it brings the theme of history and individual consciousness on the surface level. In her person, Beulah represents a force of modern sexuality, which is not only contrary to the protestant morality of Eustis but also a great threat to it. She is a modern woman without having any moral inhibitions restricting sexual conduct. Eustis sees Beulah for the first time at the pavilion on lake Jordan where he attends the services held by Brother Jimson on Easter Sunday. A group of two women and three soldiers riding noisily in a car disrupts the services and then and there Eustis sees Beulah. Two times he sees her but each time after she commits 'sin' with the soldiers.

The reaction of Eustis towards Beulah when he sees her is in keeping with the fundamental nature he holds. Looking at her he feels that if he stands close to her he "would smell the reek of sin coming off her like brimstone off the devil" (p. 87). Sex for Eustis is fornication, "sin" and those who are involved in it are devils. His perception of modern sexuality is governed by his obsession with evangelical religion and leads him to drowning the exemplary of it. Eustis sees his involvement with Beulah on religious terms. To him his infatuation with Beulah is God's will, he tells, "It was God's will I was led to her, for it was God's work I was attending when I saw her that first time" (p. 77). He finds Beulah impossible to resist and begins to see her everywhere though he tries to pray. He feels drawn to her "because a godly man feels drawn to sin every time" (p. 87). Having believed that he is at work for the Lord, Eustis had sex with Beulah in mid-May on the floor of his cotton house. He thinks he is bent upon her salvation and the only way to achieve it is through physic. Before he commits his first act of sex with Beulah, he hears the voice of God saying "Teach her what it means to be a Christian; teach her in the only way she knows" (p. 93). To Eustis, Beulah is ungodly and he has "an ache" to save her soul.

To work on his religious mission, Eustis takes Beulah to the island in the Mississippi that he remembers from his boyhood visits with his grandfather. There, as he has already thought, they live with their new names; Eustis with "Luke" Gowan and Beulah with "Sue" Gowan. The life on the island with Beulah turns sour for Eustis when he hears the life story of Miz Pitts. She tells him about her marriage, the birth of her son, Dummy and her husband's desertion of the family after he discovers that his son is deaf and dumb and his wife becomes barren. Miz Pitt's story makes Eustis think of his own situation and reminds him of his wife Kate and his young daughter Luty Pearl. That night Eustis reads the Books of Job from the Bible that Job's wife advises him to curse God and die. While he reads, Beulah watches him with reproach in her eyes, "Curse God and die, they were saying" (p. 112), he thinks. As night after night he dreams of Luty Pearl, Beulah appears to Eustis as the temptress who has tempted him to commit sin. Every time he reads the Bible, each time he thinks whether the episode in it is meant to apply to him. His mind at the moment is filled with the biblical stories of moral corruption and punishment, for example, the story of Saul's corruption and punishment, the story of Jezebel, a wicked woman and her death by the men. He is convinced that death is the only retribution for moral corruption and since Beulah represents that corruption, he waits for message from God telling to punish her.

Eustis sets himself to punish evil Beulah upon God's words saying "I'll leave it to you" (p. 123). Preoccupied with the fundamental religion of the region, Eustis sees Beulah wicked, as evil and kills her. When he is asked in the court of law by Tolliver of the cause of his killing the girl, Eustis answers that "She was wicked, evil" (p. 250). Even Dummy cannot escape the influence of the fundamental religion of the South. It affects his view of Beulah who appears to him wicked:

> Sue was like the wicked ones the prophets roared against: wore her clothes the way they did...walked the way they must have done, hip bones loose in their sockets, the bottom part of her stomach held well forward: talked the way they talked... (p. 63).

Dummy's description of Beulah corroborates Eustis's since both perceive her from the fundamental religious point of view.

Eustis's move to strangle Beulah has not only to do with the religious fundamentalism but also with his personal past. The act bears similarity with the past event related to his father's killing his wife for her promiscuous behavior. Kate, Eustis's wife and one of the narrators, explores Eustis's past in order to prove how it bears on his present. She holds the double heritage of Eustis—"Lust from the mother, murder from the father" (p. 204)—responsible for killing Beulah. His mother Lucy Dade had the appearance of "primness" but behind it there was "a promise of something unholy" (p. 198). Living by her nature Lucy, during night, slips through the frame of sash smoothed with soap to meet her lover. As she turns up pregnant, Pascal Eustis grows suspicious of her swelling stomach and runs to see whether the window is soaped as she used to do in the past to meet him. He sees the soap on the frame but waits till the baby is born. The newborn baby bears characteristic, which never does match with the elder one and then he decides to punish her. He burns his house with his wife and child in it, saving Eustis and grandfather, after cutting Lucy's throat from ear to ear, "write Hands Off across her" (p. 198), Kate describes the act.

The personal past of Eustis has shaped his mentality and he can't put it aside. The past to him is a "long straight road without bends or hills so I could stand at any point and see clear to the end" (pp. 188-89). That road begins on that night when his father wakes him up and asks him to run. By killing his wife for her unholiness, Pascal Eustis performs a Southern ritual—proneness to violence in the face of moral corruption—which Luther Eustis inherits. The legacy of violence Eustis inherits not only from his father but also from his grandfather Luther Dade who had "a share in the biggest piece of violence this country ever staged" (p. 204), Kate tells. The grandfather participated in the battle of Shiloh when he was seventeen years old losing one arm there. The influence of this old man on Eustis is so much as it is seen in his imitating the old man's actions. On the way home after he has killed Beulah, Eustis pays for ticket as his Granddaddy did:

> I paid and he gave me a cardboard stub exactly like the one Granddaddy let me hold when we came to the reunion. I put it in my hatband, the way I remembered him telling me to do... (p. 181).

That Luther Eustis lives by the past is not surprising because the past is always there stretching into the present. Eustis recalls the history of Ithaca that he heard of. He remembers how Tarfeller who wants to take revenge on his daughter's lover was killed by him and then the man was killed by Hugh Bart, the owner of the Solitaire. The event happened long back in the past but to Eustis it happened only yesterday:

> All that was before I was born, almost sixty years ago, but it might have been yesterday except for the light wires and the autos parked where the hitching-posts used to be. Nothing had really changed (p. 185).

Eustis's unwillingness to change testifies his willingness to live with the past. However, during his stay in Bristol after he kills Beulah, he doesn't let the past to enter his mind, or he doesn't dare to dream it. He tries to forget the past relating to the murder of Beulah calling it dead. He struggles to rout out the existence of the past replacing it with the present, "all there was was Now, and nothing that was past had ever been" (p. 186). But this would not ever happen. As he sees his house on his return from the island, it looks the same as always even from half a mile. He can see the lard bucket upside-down the same as two months before. Nothing is changed except that everything keeps reminding him of the past. "I asked myself was one thing after another going to keep reminding me of her all the balance of my life" (p. 187), he tells. The past will follow him down wherever and whenever he goes. This happens when he sees Dummy with policemen, he says "she came up, blocks and all" (p. 193).

Eustis's obsession with the past also has to do with the community that he is part of. In the world of novel the community is constituted of Beulah, the victim; Russell Stevenson, the reporter; Ben Rand, the circuit clerk; and Nowell Parker, the lawyer. This community tends either to have the sense of the past or partially neglects the existence of it. Beulah visits history only after she is drowned by Eustis. In her short narrative she views the past as "dead" and doesn't care to remember it. To her the only time available is the time present, as she tells, "The past is gone, time lost and dead, and.... For me, this one time is the present" (p. 125). However, as she watches the bubbles from the water, the figures from the past visit her unfolding the important events in her past life. Living in an important period of history, i.e. the great depression, Beulah was initiated in her present life by her mother. In other words, Beulah's past bears on her present life. Once initiated in the life of sex and money, she has had sexual relations with many men. When she was seventeen she was searching into the past for something that she did not know. She tells, "I could look back on my life, away back.... I was searching for something, I didn't know what, and couldn't find it" (p. 135). What she searches for is the essence of the past but she does not know it. History means nothing to her and this bars her understanding of life. As a result, sex to her is a simple fun like chewing gum or smoking or just lying on back counting stars. Although Beulah is not serious about the past, there is no doubt that, like Eustis, she is caught between the inevitable forces of history that she cannot avoid. Her encounter with Eustis may be seen as her encounter with the history; failing to understand history, she fails to understand him too.

Russell Stevenson, unlike Beulah, has a tendency of mythologizing the past. As a reporter he has an eye to look at things and his view of certain thing reveals the sense for the past. He views the jail in Bristol:

> I remember it from when I was a boy, in the days when it had a beauty only Time can bring. Its bricks were

handmade, smooth with age, cool in the hottest weather, soft as satin to the touch (p. 45).

But later, on the demand of the people, the jail was slabbed with concrete. For Stevenson it has made no difference, he says, "I'd see it and think of the brick building crouched inside, the Old South under the garish façade of the New" (p. 45). Inside the building, Stevenson observes, nothing is changed although the progressive public might slab the outer walls with concrete. The past is further mythologized in the form of the Confederate monuments. Stevenson knows one Confederate soldier tightly holding the muzzle of his gun and its base reading a message quoting from General Lee. The past is seen moving around the community in the figures of the Civil War Veterans who are not only honored but also promoted in the rank. To Eustis such figures seem "bigger than life" (p. 95) in their gray coats and hats with plumses. Even the person like Judge Holiman, who handles Eustis's case, is holding the community's sense for the past. The judge thinks he is not a part of this world since he has already retired from it and now sits to judge it. Nowell Parker, Eustis's lawyer knows it and takes advantage of the judge's love for the past.

We learn all of the lawyer's nature from the narrative of Ben Rand. He describes Nowell Parker as a man gone "sour on the world" (p. 12). The reason is, Ben Rand tells, that Nowell's wife the beautiful woman in the Delta left him for another man putting question on his "manhood". Before he turns to the criminal law, he has lived happy life of success but this life is cut short by his wife and he commences to defend the most hopeless cases of the outlaws. Defending outlaw Eustis in the court of law by putting his skill into the practice, Nowell stands against the liberalism of women in the New South of which he himself is a victim. That Nowell is not a part of the present world is revealed by his behavior. Stevenson observes him walking "with his arms held slightly away from his sides the palms turned backward like an old time gunman" (p. 54). His is the world of the past of classical music of Mozart and Haydn, of literature by Keats, Browning, especially by Shakespeare. He lives in "the big old house" built by his grandfather and if one passes by it at night hears "highbrow music" (p. 12). The arts—music and literature—is Nowell's escape from the contemporary world. His distaste to technological development is expressed in his remarks. As he walks down to Marshall Avenue, he looks at the sun and then checks his watch saying that "We've progressed so far in our mechanistic materialism that now we look at our watches to check on the sun" (p. 220).

Nowell's knowledge of literature and the classical music offers him a perspective to judge the present. Having heard the story of Eustis's wife, Kate, Nowell sees its occurrence in an "atmosphere" similar to that of a play by Shakespeare. Nowell tells, "What she told me had occurred in an atmosphere much like that of *Triolus and Cressida*, in which the faithful are betrayed and the brave are slain" (p. 219). Similarly, listening to the story of Beulah told by Eustis, Nowell says he is reminded of the words of the Duke in *Measure for Measure:*

> ... I have seen corruption boil and bubble
> Till it o'er-run the stew... (p. 229).

Nowell's habits of realizing the present in relation to the past in a literary text helps him to understand the men and women around him. He is a lawyer-historian who seeks the root cause of the problem of his clients in order to judge them. He learns the past of his client Eustis and also of Miz Pitts and that of Beulah to realize of their present lives. What he learns from their pasts is that they are victims of the circumstance, which is born due to the defeat in the Civil War. The biographies of these characters, including his own, to Nowell, are all alike because they are "histories of inadequacy" marked by "the failure of Love" which is traceable to the event of the Civil War:

> Love has failed us. We are essentially, irrevocably alone. Anything that seems to combat that loneliness is a trap—Love is a trap: Love has failed us in this century. We left our better destiny in '65, defeated though we fought with a fury that seems to indicate foreknowledge of what would follow if we lost. Probably it happened even earlier: maybe in Jackson's time. Anyhow—

> whenever—we left the well springs, and ever since then we have been moving toward this ultimate failure of nerve (p. 223).

In Nowell's view, the ills of the New South have their roots in the defeat of the Old South and must be understood in historical context. The promiscuity of Nowell's wife and that of Beulah can be realized by referring to the Southern past. Defeat in the Civil War puts question on the South's manhood since the Southerners have failed to protect their land and women. Its result is the liberation of the Southern women from the role traditionally assigned to them. Nowell's wife leaves him for another man, putting question on his manhood. Eustis refers to his manhood when he fails to perform sex with Kate the night following the day of his return. The other characters, too, share the same historical fate. Lonzo, the photographer, is homosexual; Stevenson has no wife and thinks not to have one. The South has lost its manhood in the Civil War and thereupon sex failed in the region. Nowell's perception of ills of the New South in the light of Southern past not only separates him from the average Bristolite but also gives him upper hand over them.

Nowell is bent upon saving Eustis, for he is a victim of the forces of history beyond his control. He knows that people hate Eustis because they cannot comprehend him, so it is his duty to make the jurors think that they can understand him. And he has to do it in a simple way for complicated way will lose the case. The simple way is to "Make them believe he was insane and the scales would fall from their eyes: they would 'understand'; the fear, the hate would be gone, evaporated" (p. 237). In his attempt to prove Eustis's insanity, Nowell presents the testimony of Dr. Goodnight, a psychiatrist, in which he has admitted Eustis's madness. His testimony comes as a judgment on Nowell's suppositions of a man reading the Bible all the time even stopping his plow to read it and thinking to cut his throat with a razor because he is obsessed with sin. The second testimony of Eustis's madness comes from Miz Pitts who tells that "he's is a good man that got pulled into something by a bad girl because he's a little crazy" (p. 19).

By these testimonies, Nowell convinces the jury that things done in a state of preoccupation with something is a fanaticism, a form of madness hence undeserving the capital punishment. Eustis's preoccupation with the religious fundamentalism is judged as madness in modern times. However, Nowell Parker perceives Eustis's madness as the disease of the entire Southern culture.

In his next and the third novel, *Love in a Dry Season** (1951) Foote's inclination towards Southern history becomes more and more outstanding. In this novel, he offers a set of central characters who are perceived on the basis of their relation to the South's chivalrous tradition and the values which go along with it. Living in a crucial time of change, the characters in the novel are failed because either they are obsessed with the past or hopelessly confused with the values of the past. Major Malcolm Barcroft's preoccupation with the past Confederate heroism not only excludes him from the present but also fails him in his role as a father. Jeff and Amy Carruthers, too, fail to live as husband and wife because their relationship is devoid of the past values. The lovers, Amanda Barcroft and Harley Drew, also fail in their love since the love they enact is never defined by history and tradition hence doomed to fail. In a sense, the relationship fail the characters in *Love in a Dry Season* because love, which sustains the relationships, fails to grow in a season which is dry in historical sense. The failure of Southern characters in modern times, to Foote, is due to the decadence of the Old order in which men, who lived by the code, were certain of their goals. As there is no sense of that order, the character like Amy lives by "instinct" or like Jeff who lives by "subterfuge". On the other side there is Major Barcroft with his "courteous old-world manner" (p. 3) living his static life.

At the outset of the novel, the narrator introduces the character of Major Barcroft as one having mighty sense of history but lacking human sensitivity. Born during the

---

* Shelby Foote, *Love in a Dry Season* (New York: Random House, 1979). All subsequent references in the text are to this edition.

Reconstruction in the house of a Confederate officer, the Major is reared on the line of the Confederate heroic tradition. As a boy, he attends military school in Tennessee where he finds interest of his talent. During vacation at home, he reads military biographies and develops, as the narrator says, "the habit of saying, 'Good, good', as Stonewall Jackson was said to have done" (p. 4). In his final year at Tennessee, he decides on military career soon after he is appointed as a cadet captain. He even looks forward to doing his duty at the frontier, or in Washington, or, above all, in "a real war to lodge his name in the history books, or at least in the tactics manuals" (p. 4). However, the Major can't continue his military education further due to financial crisis in his family and he returns home only to take job of a cotton broker in his uncle's office. Though he settles well in business, his preoccupation with the military tradition remains intact. Having inherited half a million dollars in securities, the Major is in a position to have anything he asks for, except, the narrator tells, "the very one thing he wanted most: a male heir" (p. 6). Like Luther Eustis in *Follow Me Down*, the Major wants a male child to retain the military tradition of the family and when his wife has borne him two daughters consecutively, he is not as happy as he is when she has borne him a son next time. The Major's wife wants to name the child Hezekiah but, since she is no more, the Major calls him Malcolm "the name of the first born male Barcroft for five generations now" (p. 6).

The aura of the confederate heroism clutches Major Barcroft all through his life. In the seat of his mind, he carries a "dream of martial fame" (p. 6) and during the Spanish-American War the dream is near to be fulfilled when he is given a commission. But the war ends before his regiment embarks and he retires with the rank of Major. He undertakes raising of his only son in order to make him a soldier as his pattern demands. He starts giving him lessons of riding a horse and practically asks him to sit in the saddle of the Shetland pony he has given him for the purpose. But the son is not as enthusiastic as the father and being effeminate in manner, he is frightened by it and falls ill. Then the Major, trying other ways, brings a crate of lead soldiers, infact miniature warriors each with its musket or saber. The Major tells his son that it is his army and starts to teach him how to play it by demarking the positions held by General Lee and Stonewall Jackson. He teaches his son that war is "terrible" yet "we should grow too fond of it" (p. 8). In the Major's persons the past is internalized consequently he fights the Civil War in his mind. It is made clear in the narrator's comment on the Major's absorption in demonstrating the tactics of Fredericksburg where he forgets that, the narrator tells, "the demonstration was intended for his son" (p. 9). The Barcroft military tradition ends abruptly when Malcolm is accidentally killed in hunting game by a companion with the shotgun the Major has given. History embodied in Southern military tradition fails Major Barcroft.

Even after Malcolm's death, the Major's obsession with the Confederate military tradition continues unabated. During the First World War, he goes to New Orleans to volunteer for active service in the war. He is forty-four and will likely get a desk job but he thinks that once he is admitted and he is in uniform "he could manage to get himself assigned to duty with troops in the field" (p. 15). Here, too, the glory of war escapes the Major since the heart murmur prevents him from securing admission in the war. All his life the Major intensely wants to prove himself as a soldier and he will do anything for it. Even an outsider like Harley Drew can see the Major's intense obsession with military glory and what move he may take to achieve it. As a response to Amy's question, Drew tells her that he has "moderately scared" in the war and still two years of the war is "the best time" of his life because, he tells, "I know an old man lives on Lamar Street would sell his soul for ten minutes of what I had almost two years of" (p. 209). It is war that excites the Major all and when the Second World War breaks out, he is seen busy in pricking pins to mark the position of the armies on a large-scale map of western Europe. Irrespective of his chest pain, he wants to "look at his map in peace" (p. 176), and wait for pain to stop. When the Major is convalescing at home, he reads the war news and directs his daughter, Amanda, where to place pins on the map. When she cannot locate the French and Belgian border helmets, he becomes furious.

The Major's preoccupation with the heroic past and his failure to follow that past deeply affects his relationship with his daughters, Florence and Amanda. His behavior toward his maiden daughters is not like that of a father but of a frustrated man having no affection at all for any human creature. Stern and rigid by nature, the Major's presence fills their minds with fear. Malcom's death frightens the sisters because it comes at a time when they have just begun to be invited to ice cream parties. But what frightens them most of all is their father's face that the narrator describes as "at once stern and unyielding and yet at the same time ravaged" (p. 11). The Major's devotion to a definite pattern makes him send the girls to Catholic convent school since the public school is not considered "nice". In the school, the elder sister Florence develops asthma that changes her and her sister's life way separating them both from the world they have just begun to know. The Major keeps the high school principal, Mr. Rosenbach to give his daughters private lessons but it is not good for them since "they were terrified" (p. 13) of the principal. In fact the sisters are barricaded in the big gray house on Lamar Street "seated by their window in the darkness, the Barcroft girls had more to overhear than the ice-cream parties and kissing games" (pp. 13-14), the narrator tells. They imagine, even identify the sliding feet of their former schoolmates dancing with music at the Elysian Club three blocks away from their big house.

The world of the two sisters is divided as Florence stops sharing the second-story bedroom with Amanda to avoid exertion and moves to ground-floor room. Away from her sister in an airtight room, Florence begins to see nightmares of snakes and galloping horses. The Major comes to her room every evening to see her but, the narrator says, "Florence was afraid of him; he so obviously represented the outside world against which she had built her barricade" (p. 15). Florence is denied not only the fatherly love but also the pride that the young women of her age take in their possessions. When she, out of pretense, complains that her long hair makes her uncomfortably hot, the Major arranges Sam Marino, his regular barber, to cut it. What she actually means is not that the hair really bothers her, but being proud of it, it is her way to call attention to it. The Major, on the contrary despises boasting or any pretense covering boasting because he has nothing in his life to boast of. "He despised boasting", the narrator tells, "never having needed to boast himself; most of all he despised any pretense that was meant to cover boasting" (p. 15). He wants Florence to admit her pretense and when she persists in it, the Major asks the barber to cut her hair in order to teach her "a lesson on the evils of pretense" (p. 18). Sam Marino, who sees something is wrong about the house, comments on the father's behavior on the occasion saying that "discipline had come to resemble cruelty" (p. 18). After the hair-cutting incident, Florence develops a nightmare in which she sees her being sexually attacked by her father. Her father's visit to her room, twice a week now, is no more comforting to her; during the time he is with her "she sat with her knees pressed close together, like a woman in fear of assault" (p. 20).

Florence falls prey to her father's anger aroused out of his failure to prove himself as a soldier. Losing his last chance at military glory, the Major becomes vindictive and it is during the war that, when "his manner was short with everyone" (p. 16), Florence pretentiously complains of her long hair. Her madness can be considered as her refuse from angry and violent world constituted mainly of her father. Unable to come out of the confinement herself, Florence will like to see Amanda free from it so she asks Harley Drew to take Amanda away from "this terrible house". But Amanda can't be freed as she is encircled by her angry father and asthmatic sister. She comes out of the circle, temporarily, when Harley Drew enters her life as a lover. Driven by her emotional need, Amanda surrenders herself to him without giving any thought to his motive. The lovers, Amanda and Drew, decide to marry but the Major refuses it on the ground that Drew cannot tell the color of Amanda's eyes. Next time, the lovers plan to run away but the Major senses the plan and threatens Amanda that he will disinherit her if she does so, and also makes her realize her responsibility toward Florence. It is only after death, for Amanda the death of Florence and for Drew the death of the Major, that the marriage seems possible so the lovers have to wait. During the years of their waiting, the walks with Drew have carried Amanda through the time, so his desertion of Amanda breaks her and leaves her incapable to love other as well. Just after the renouncement, Amanda can't hold herself and she burst out crying. When she sees her father approaching, she thinks his features have gone softer and, as the narrator tells, "she had an impulse to hurry to him, to throw herself into his arms for comfort" (p. 172). Then she realizes that the softness was due to her tears in her eyes, and not from the Major's expression. She sees his face becoming sterner and sterner as he asks her "Go to your room. Don't sit there crying like that" (p. 172).

The Major never cares Amanda's feelings as well as never tries to communicate with her to know about them. He does not think necessary to speak to her on such occasions as when he denies Drew's proposal of marriage and when Drew abandons Amanda. Whatever communication that has been there between the father and the daughter before, it is failed after the renouncement. "Formerly he had spoken to her but seldom; now he never spoke to her at all, beyond signifying incidental desires with grunts and gestures" (p. 179), the narrator observes. Though the daughter and the father walk together, from the office to the house, "they were as uncommunicative as soldiers on parade" (p. 179). The Major judges things on a definite pattern and when the things do not go by the pattern, he rejects them. Drew's proposal of marriage with Amanda is rejected because Drew can't remember the color of Amanda's eyes. In fact the Major has no illusion of Drew's motive and thinks better to reject it. When the Major sees Amanda crying after Drew leaves her, he is "angry because a Barcroft had been humbled" (p. 172) for the first time. However, the Major will like to see Amanda married by the pattern, so he brings Henry Stublefield, a new business associate and childless widower to court Amanda. He is, as the narrator describes, a "cavalier, Old South", "gallant" (p. 181). To Amanda he resembles Drew and, inspite of her father's encouragement, she rejects Henry's silent proposal with the word "Don't". Since the things do not go as he wants them go, the Major abandons all concern about her saying "I give you up, Amanda. Ive tried: God knows Ive tried" (p. 187). Rejected both by her lover and her father, Amanda is utterly alone with Florence's malady of bad dream that she inherits. Her dream is suggestive of the denial of access to sexual pleasure by her father.

After her father's death, alone in the big house, Amanda is haunted by the recent past. The "lofty rooms" of the big house are filled with memories of the dead—the memories of the "stern father" and "invalid sister". The past returns to her as she hears screams of dead Florence or talks to herself to go to meet her father who is already dead. Her obsession with the past, and loneliness as well, lead her to the reading of the novels by the great writers. In their novels, the narrator tells, "she read her own story without recognition. She did not think while she read; she lived" (p. 241). In her own person, Amanda retains the old order represented by her father. Her striking resemblance with her father is always emphasized; despite of Drew's winning her heart, to the people of Bristol "she was her father's daughter" (p. 143). Toward the end of the novel, the narrator calls our attention to Amanda's resemblance to her father. She wears pince-nez with fine gold chain like her father and her gray hair, the narrator tells, "caused people to remark how much she had come to resemble Major Barcroft" (p. 249). Amanda wins the combat against loneliness when she joins the church which gives her "the sense of belonging" (p. 234). Though Amanda sells her father's house, which is a reminder of the past, she retains the old order by joining the Episcopal Church and the Red Cross, thus she, unlike Jeff and Amy Carruthers, sticks to the past moorings.

Jeft and Amy Carruthers fail to live happily as husband and wife because they have lost their moorings in the past.

Ignorant of the tradition constituted of morals and manners, they are confused with the roles the marriage assigns to them. Their marriage is not the result of affection between the two but of a series of perversions. They are cousins who grow up spending summers together at the family home near Myrtle Beach. Jeff who has affection for pornography, spends his summer watching Amy and her beau perform on the front porch-swing at the country house. Jeff thinks it better than the comic books or sometime strangely like them. Once he gets the chance in swing when Amy's beau fails to come but "at the critical moment he panicked; he was terrified; he even began to weep" (p. 36), the narrator tells. Later, in other summers, Amy does not allow Jeff to have such intimacy again so he stands outside the bathroom door when Amy is inside bathing and listens to "the splash of water, the flop of a soapy washcloth" (p. 37). The distant listening follows actual watching when Jeff, knowing that Amy never turns the key, enters the bathroom only to be stricken by her. Amy's manner with Jeff, who is three years younger than her, as the narrator says, "had been more that of a riding instructor than a lover, let alone a maiden in submission" (p. 37). To Jeff it is "terribly unmanly" so that he looks for a time "when he could repay her, could laugh at her or strike her as he saw fit" (p. 38).

Thus, Jeff marries Amy because he wants to repay her what she has given him and Amy marries him because she desires no serious "change in her life" as there will be if she marries other than Jeff. Essentially the marriage tends to stormy and the quarrels between the two begin soon after they have married. Jeff's "sense of inadequacy" takes the form of jealousy; he becomes jealous of Amy's infidelity. In reality Jeff does not want to object her infidelity; "he desired it in fact", the narrator tells, "provided she would let him watch" (p. 42). Jeff wants to be a husband and a voyeur at the same time, but he can't be either since the accident makes him blind and impotent as well. After the accident it is Amy who makes advances in the bed but, the narrator tells, "there was no response, no resurrection of the flesh" (p. 45). The word "resurrection" brings to mind that Jeff's, what Phillips,

Jr. says, "sensibilities had lost their moorings in both history and the natural world, and there was nothing to restore them".[2] Cut off from history that guides man, Jeff has confused the role of a husband with a role of a voyeur. Being blind, he is unable to satisfy his voyeuristic compulsion therefore he resents Amy's unfaithfulness through violence. At Briertree, a large plantation house, the relationship between Jeff and Amy is characterized by, what the narrator says, "enmity round the clock" (p. 49). It is here at Briertree that Jeff's new identity comes to light, i.e., homosexual which even causes to arouse sexual jealousy in Amy. Jeff's attachment with Harley Drew is built upon his homosexual need which Amy perceives by her "intuition". As Drew develops his affair with Amy, the attachment between them breaks and it is replaced by jealousy when Jeff comes to know Drew's affair with Amy. There is no doubt that Jeff's jealousy of Drew is double-sided when he shoots him. The deterioration of Jeff's manhood is complete toward the end of the novel when the narrator says Jeff resembles eunuch, "or rather the classic conception of a eunuch—as if the knife sharp silver of windshield glass had performed a physical as well as psychological castration" (p. 291). One thing be noted here that with Jeff, Amy always plays as a castrating woman and her role in his castration never be neglected.

Amy Carruther's first appearance in the novel leaves an impression of her type: New Southern woman. She is seen in her semi-transparent dress "which allowed the pink of her nipples to show through" (p. 30). She wears no brassier and no undergarment of any sort. "There was no modesty about her" (p. 30), the narrator tells. Her movements are so slow and lazy that the people watching her think that she is preserving her energy for "something she really cared about—bed" (p. 30). On occasions she does not mind being watched rather she likes it. Three years older than Jeff, Amy always had an upper hand on him before as well as after marriage. In spite of Jeff's impotency and blindness, Amy lives with him not because she is retaining the marital bond but because it gives her an advantage in her affair with the other people. The narrator tells that "she could tell herself she was 'sticking by him', and it was especially advantageous when something like the Perkins affair came up" (p. 49). She was engaged in a series of affair outside marriage with others. Her endless desire for 'change' drives her to search for a new sexual partner when she is bored with the first one. First she seeks Perkins then, during the tour in Europe, she is involved with a series of men such as ski-instructor, the Spaniard and then back home, she seeks Harley Drew. Amy becomes so bold in her affair with Drew that she prefers to have sex with him under the blind man's nose. The affair with Drew ends as Jeff raids the bedroom of the lovers and punishes them, however, Amy already begins to loose her interest in Harley Drew. Amy's desire for change has strongly to do with what the narrator calls "her essential promiscuity" (p. 211). Sex is a play and not ritual to Amy. Loosened from the moorings embodied in Briartree, Amy is washed away in the flood of change only to be drowned.

That Amy has lost the sense of the past is obvious in her outlook on Briartree her great grandfather had built on the shores of Lake Jordan in 1857. She moves there not because she has any desire but because she thinks the notion romantic. The practical reasons behind it are that her affair with Perkins is "on the wane" and she has developed enmity for Jeff who kills her pet dog. To Amy, her returning to Briartree is "a sort of pilgrimage to hallowed ground, the blind seed swimming home" (p. 32). It is true that Amy is a "blind seed" and though she restores Briartree to "all its Original glory" (p. 46) she lacks insight to realize what it stands for. It never occurs to Amy that inheritance implies heritage one must live by. At Briartree Amy is "the mistress", "the chatelaine" and successor to those old women who ran the house efficiently, and who, as the narrator tells, "wore clothes that gave inch for inch as much covering as armor" (p. 50). They were not only "willowy and tender" but also bore number of children and raised them according to "formula". In the Old time, Amy would have been "Old Miss" and Jeff would have been "Mars Jeff" living among the men who lived by "singleness of purpose" and whose "cult was cotton" (p. 50). But the lives of Amy and Jeff do not coincide with the lives of those who lived at Briartree. Their failure to assume their heritage parallels the failure of Amy's grandfather, Cass Tarfeller to do so. Having challenged a gambler, who has defiled his daughter, for the duel, Tarfeller is killed by his opponent because of, as the narrator makes clear, "his belated assumption of a heritage for which he had never been fit" (p. 27). Having no sense of the past, lives of Amy and Jeff become increasingly violent. First there is killing of a dog, then there is a man whom Jeff tries to shoot in a hotel near Nice, and then there is, first, Harley Drew whom Jeff shoots to kill, second, Amy whose face Jeff smashes to the point of ugliness.

Harley Drew provides the third dimension to the relationship in the novel, i.e., lover. He is not a romantic courting lover in the old sense but an emissary of the world of finance whom love is a business. He presents himself as a lover to Amanda Barcroft because, as the narrator tells, "he fixed his mind on the million-dollar purse" (p. 74). Keeping an eye on the Major's fortune, Drew easily attaches to Amanda. When the Major refuses his proposal of marriage, Drew resolves to wait till the death of Florence and the Major. "It would be necessary to stay", Drew thinks, "to protect his investment" (p. 96). Similarly, Drew's courtship of Amy Carruther is based on the financial consideration. Being financial advisor, he knows the Carruther's estate which is twice in size of the Major's holdings and it is the reason for which he deserts Amanda. What he wants is Jeff's money and Jeff's wife so he plans to eliminate the husband. Paradoxically, it is Jeff who has almost killed him but he is saved. Convulsing in a hospital, Drew learns the Major's death and the speculation on size of his estate. At first he feels regretted, then he thinks that everything is not lost and as for Amanda is concerned, he can make up the things. He plans to kneel down before her and will shed some tears, and when he thinks how his plan is "his spirit rose in ratio to the estimates of Major Barcroft's fortune" (p. 230). Towards the end of the novel, Drew marries the widow of a cosmetics manufacturer twelve years older than him. She brings him not only wealth but also high social position which he strives for from the beginning. The three characters, Drew, Jeff, and Amy, show to what extent the Southern society is degenerated due to lack of sense of the past.

Foote's fourth novel *Shiloh** (1952) shows how the Southerner's psychic affinity with the past leads them into defeat in the battle at the Shiloh. It is a crucial battle in the series of the Civil War fought between the high-spirited, romantic-minded Southern forces and well-trained, mechanical minded Northern forces. The novel is more an analysis of the Southern mind and less an account of the battle. And there is no better way to analyze it than juxtaposing it with the Northern mind. For that matter, Foote crowds the novel with many character-narrators from both sides, the Confederate as well as the Union, and offers the reader a comparative access to the characters. The men who speak for the Union side include Captain Fountain, Private Flickner and twelve members of a squad from the 23rd Indiana Regiment. Those who speak for the Confederate side are Lieutenant Metcalfe, Private Dade, and Sergeant Polly. By alternating their narratives, Foote delineates the Southern character in relation with the Northern one. There is no doubt that Foote's interest lies in the Southern character since the Southern narrators and the Southern cause dominate the novel. The Southern men take ample space to narrate their experiences in the battle than those Northerners do. It is a Southerner who opens and closes the novel. The Northerners are used only to provide a counterpoint to the Southerners. In fine, what the novel reveals is that the Northerners never bother about the past and the Southerners, on the other hand, use the past to pattern the present.

The past has deeper meaning for Lieutenant Palmer Metcalfe, a Southerner who begins the novel. His narrative is comprehensive because his sense of the past enables him to provide necessary information required of him as a narrator. He knows a great deal about Albert Sidney Johnston, a

---

* Shelby Foote, *Shiloh* (New York: The Dial Press, 1952). All subsequent references in the text are to this edition.

commander of the Confederate Army of Mississippi, from his father who has been so close a friend to Johnston as to serve as a second in Johnstan's duel with Felix Huston. His father has followed Johnston through wars in Texas and Mexico and now nineteen years old son, Metcalfe serves as a junior officer on Johnstan's staff. In a sense, his serving under Johnston is repeating the past of his own father. However, it is not all, the past comes to him time to time. Lying sleepless on the ground the Saturday night before the battle, the past wells up in his consciousness and he sees the images of his father and mother. He thinks of his father as a soldier who lost his one arm in Texas war fighting under the command of Johnston and of his mother who has died soon after he is born. Whatever he knows about her is from "a Sully portrait" of her and her clothes stored in the attic. Looking at her portrait, Metcalfe once calls her "bride of quietness" because she looks immortal like the girl, Keats describes in his ode. He looks back at his parents' life, which seems strange to him, particularly the way they "met and loved and gone through all that joy and pain" (p. 26). As the past of his parents melts, the past regarding Sherman predicting the fall of the Confederacy floats into Metcalfe's mind.

At the Louisiana State Military Academy, Metcalfe, the student, overhears Sherman, the superintendent, reacting to the news of South Carolina's secession. Metcalfe has heard Sherman say "You are bound to fail. Only in your spirit and determination are you prepared for war. In all else you are totally unprepared, with a bad cause to start with" (p. 217). Sherman knows that the people of the South, along with their cause are bound to fail since they are engaged in fighting with "the most powerful, ingeniously mechanical and determined people" (p. 217) of the North. Sherman views the battle as a conflict between Agrarian South and Commercial North. The figure of Sherman uttering words of Southerners' failure comes to Metcalfe throughout the first year of the war. It comes to him in the war at Bowling Green and Donelson, during the retreat from Kentucky to Mississippi, and not to mention, it comes to him at the Shiloh. It is the past of the fatality of the

Southern cause that Metcalfe never wants to come to terms with. When it comes to him, he becomes restless and sees the vision of his making Sherman admit, at the point of pistol, that he is wrong. He tries to find out the answer which will prove Sherman false and that he finds it in the person of Forrest. Retreating with his weary men, Forrest turns on the pursuing Northerners at the Fallen Timbers and sends them back "demoralized". Metcalfe reflects that the army that has Forrest can trust in something beside "mechanical aptitude" Sherman talks about. "This was the answer to all he had said" (p. 218), Metcalfe tells. He upholds superiority of the Southern individualism over the mechanical people of the North forgetting what his father says of the Southern character bearing within it the seeds of defeat.

The death of Johnston reminds Metcalfe of his father's reflection on the Southern cause and Southern temperament, which is similar to that of Sherman's. Others have told Metcalfe how Johnston, just before he is hit in the leg, has ordered his surgeon, Dr. Yandell, to treat the wounds of a group of captured Federal soldiers. When the doctor protests, Johnston kills him leaving no one to treat him after he gets wounded. Having heard that the general has died because of his concern for the wounded enemy, Metcalfe remembers his father's words:

> I remembered what my father had said about the South bearing within itself the seeds of defeat, the Confederacy being conceived already moribund. We were sick from an old malady, he said: incurable romanticism and misplaced chivalry, too much Walter Scott and Dumas read too seriously. We were in love with the past, he said; in love with death (p. 200).

Metcalfe's father foresees defeat of the Southern cause, which for him lies not in outside factors but in the Southern character itself. His analysis of the Southern character greatly emphasizes the theme of history and individual consciousness in the novel, and for Metcalfe, it brings the fact into light that defeat in the battle has its origin in Southernmen. Ironically, what Metcalfe's father says of the Southern character is as applicable to his own person as it does to his son and other southern characters in the novel.

It is obvious that Metcalfe's father is sick from romanticism in spite of his posing himself as a "realist" and a "straight thinker". Metcalfe reveals that his father was "a highly romantic figure of a man himself and he knew it" (p. 200). He carries around his person a romantic aura displayed in his tales of war in Texas, in his scars of war on his forehead and his empty sleeve, and in his midnight drinking under the portrait of his dead wife. He talks in a realistic way because there is an urge in him for "self-destruction" and hate for his old age. He sends his son to a war because he is unable to take part in it himself. Metcalfe says that his father's action is motivated by a "regret of a particular regional form" (p. 200). The son, Metcalfe, who knows the reality about his father's situation, fails to keep himself away from his father's malady. He repeats his father's romanticism as he decides to join the cavalry of the romantic warrior Forrest. His decision comes after he witnesses Forrest's incomparable bravery in the battlefield. Metcalfe sees him alone charging at the enemy soldiers fifty yards away from his cavalry. When they surround Forrest, he makes his way back, grabs up one enemy soldier and dashes him against a jagged stump as he rejoins his men. It is breath-taking experience for Metcalfe that he has had of such kind never before. He thinks to leave the staff work and decides to enlist under Forrest after Shiloh. It doesn't matter what reality Metcalfe confronts, he, like his father, cannot resist the lure of romance; both the father and the son are "incurable" romanticists. In their cases history proves to be irresistible.

Metcalfe is not only preoccupied with his personal and regional past but also, beyond that, a European past. He works with Colonel Jordan on a battle order using Napoleon's Waterloo tactics as a guide. He is so conscious of his share in the preparation of battle order that he calls himself, as he tells, "a latter-day Shakespeare because I had supplied the commas and semicolons" (p. 205). It seems so beautiful to him that he ranks Colonel Jordan with Napoleon. He is confident of its result and thinks if it is followed closely, it will result in victory. When the work is finished, Metcalfe ranks it among creative art as produced by Shakespeare, as he says, "I began to understand how Shakespeare must have felt when he finished *Macbeth*" (p. 13). Later as the battle plan fails, Metcalfe admits that it is faulty, it is perfect on paper but never so when put it in practice. Their strategy of victory turns out a blueprint for their defeat. Metcalfe has time to reflect upon their battle plan when he lies there under "tattered sky" thinking that the "main fault lay in the battle order I had helped to prepare" (p. 205). The past is useless in giving them victory in the present war. The negative result of the battle plan, Metcalfe observes, is the loss of coordination between soldiers and their commanders. Following instructions taught by their superiors, the divisions and regiments are so intermingled that the commanding officers have lost contact with their men. At that time some lines of *Macbeth* cross Metcalfe's mind:

> We but teach
> Bloody instructions, which being taught, return
> To plague th'inventor (p. 206).

The past proves to be a boomerang to Metcalfe and his fellow-Southerners as it does to Macbeth in the play. In a sense, fighting war on Napoleon's battle order is an attempt, on the part of the Southerners, to live by the time past in the present.

The two narratives—put at the beginning and ending—of Metcalfe are important thematically since they provide the reader with an analysis of the Southern character that causes defeat in the battle. The reason of the Southerners being at the Shiloh, to Foote, is their reading Scott's romances too seriously. What is imaginative, they have taken as true and have adopted chivalry as a code of their life. Their preoccupation with the code makes the Southerners what they are not—soldiers. Metcalfe observes that most of the soldiers are untrained and using the weapons for the first time. When they march, which they do for the first time, they march with a "holiday air". The romantic behavior of the soldiers is further revealed when the sun comes out Saturday evening before the battle. They begin to shoot at birds and rabbits along the way without minding the enemy outposts two miles away. Those are Tennessee troops who, proud of their marksmanship, starts shooting at a small buck "but so far as I could tell, not a ball came within ten feet of that buck" (p. 24), Metcalfe tells. Likewise the men from the Orleans Guard battalion come to the battle wearing parade dress of blue color that the enemy wear. The Confederates mistake them for Federals and shoot at them. They promptly return it and when a staff officer goes there and tells them that they are shooting at their friends, the colonel says "I know it, Sir, but damnit we fire on everybody who fires on us!" (p. 204). The pervasive influence of Scott's romanticism on their minds makes Southerners consider war not seriously.

The romantic idealism has its spell on Private Luther Dade too. He is a rifleman attached to the 6th Mississippi and also serves as the second narrator on the Southern side. He joins army because General Beauregard has appealed for "true men" to "save the country". He has a plan to return home "with a Yankee sword for the fireplace, like pa did with the Mexican one" (p. 64). Luther Dade's devotion to the Southern cause is also governed by the romantic ideal, which sustains through the battle. There are moments, of course, during the battle in which he comes to reality but only momentarily. His experience of war is so discouraging that he thinks "Luther, you got no business mixed up in all this ruckus. This is all crazy, I thought" (p. 75). But he comes out of this thought quickly and next moment becomes a part of the 6th Mississippi that throws itself to destruction. They yell as they run and this time the racket is louder because, Luther Dade tells, "I was yelling too, crazy and blood-curdled as the rest of them" (p. 77). Even the wound in his arm does not shake him from his ideal and he tells Captain Plummer that the wound doesn't hurt him except he can't lift his hand up. Towards the end of the novel Luther Dade is cured of his romantic ideal as there is no victory to provide escape. Lying wounded in the wagon, he sees the column of army heading for Corinth and he asks Metcalfe, "Lieutenant did we get whupped?" (p. 222). Luther

Dade's experience of war can be seen as representative of those Southerners who have devoted to the Southern Cause. Defeat is a new beginning for the Southerners, it is a coming to experience from innocence. "It was like being born again, coming into a new world" (p. 75), Luther Dade says. Even both Metcalfe and Polly noted the change in him.

Sergeant Jefferson Polly, the third narrator who speaks for the Confederates, has a past that he thinks important. Polly's father, a Baptist minister in Houston, Texas, plans to make his son a minister like him but Polly is rather unwilling. His father is disillusioned when he hears from the head of the divinity school in Baltimore about Polly and his roommate are caught with a girl and bottles of whiskey. It ends his career as minister but he is happy because, as he tells, "It meant an end to trying to be something I was never meant to be" (pp. 147-48). For six years following the fiasco, Polly has tried many jobs such as a sailor, a card dealer, a cowboy and a field hand. In Galveston, he thinks to go to his father but the war comes and he decides instead to join the Confederate navy. However, he changes his mind as he reads Forrest's advertisement for volunteers in a newspaper in Memphis and joins Forrest's cavalry. Polly has not only the sense of his own past but also knows the past of Forrest. He tells that people are spreading "the legend" when they say about Forrest's coming into the war barefoot. For Polly knows Forrest's past is different from the legend people are spreading. Born in a family of blacksmith, Forrest has lost his father when he was sixteen years old. He grows up working with his uncle in livery stable and when he becomes twenty-four, he marries a girl, Mary Ann. Forrest is very successful in his livestock trade that enables him to become a man of a million-dollar and of five thousand acres of plantation land. People esteem Forrest to be worthy of their trust and elect him to the Board of Alderman three times. So what the people say of Forrest being illiterate, is all false, Polly narrates.

Polly has fought with Forrest from the beginning of the war and the Colonel had become his hero. "I followed him and watched him grow to be what he had become by the time of Shiloh: the first cavalryman of his time" (p. 150), Polly says. In the present battle seeing the reinforcement that will bring victory for the Union, Polly and Forrest know that the night attack will be the only chance for the Confederate army. As it turns out that they find no General in Southern army who is willing to attack in the night in spite of Forrest's warning of their defeat in the morning. Polly's observations of the battle are that of a seasoned scout who can see flaws in the Southern battle order based on Napoleon's one. There are no specific orders for the Colonels so that the man like Forrest doesn't know where he is required and similarly the aids to the officials do not think it unusual, and they say that this is a way to fight battle. To Polly, it seems strange, as he says. "That seemed to me to be a mighty loose-jointed way to fight a war" (p. 142). On the other side, Polly sees the Federals are more planned, organized in their attack and they know that cavalry is useless at the Shiloh which, Polly says, none of Forrest's men realize. From the observations of Polly, it appears that the Southerners are engaged in battle not for victory but mostly for their defeat. The confusion on the battlefield is symptomatic of Southerners' confusion with history—a European past—as a pattern for the present. The Northerners on the other hand, are not confused for they never judge the present with the past.

The first narrator on the Northern side is Captain Walter Fountain, Adjutant, 53rd Ohio, who provides background, as Metcalfe does, leading up to the battle. Past is not important to Fountain as it does to his Southern counterparts and though he knows the past of Grant, it serves him as informative and not as connective between their characters. He knows about Grant, it is because they have come from the same town, Georgetown where Fountain has watched Grant drill militia. Rest of his knowledge about Grant's past comes only from hearing people talk about him. Fountain does not share the past of his General; neither is it common thread between them. When he tells Grant's life story, he is more detached than involved. However, he has confidence in his General, as he says, "Fighting under Grant meant winning victories" (p. 47). For Fountain the reason of the present war lies in the difference between the Southerners' and Northerners' ways of life, as he tells, "There were hotheads in the South who thought more of their Negroes and their pride than they did of their country" (p. 40). But when it comes to defend their ways, the Southerners do not show their ability as they boast: one Southern volunteer is worth of ten Yankee soldiers. Being not preoccupied with any past, Fountain can see the battle with clear consciousness.

Among the Northerners, the man who comments on the past is Private Otto Flickner but his comments are for the denial rather than for acceptance of the past. Flickner's father tells Flickner tales of the grandfather's having fought against Napoleon, but to Flickner tales of the past are useless, mostly dead. "This is a new country. We don't need those stories from the old one" (p. 112), he tells his father. He also thinks that his father's tales of the old country are "out of place" in this new country. Although Flickner carries the watch that his grandfather had worn when he fought Napoleon, the time it stands for doesn't matter him. Fighting against the Confederates, Flickner also sees the difference between the men of two regions saying that the Southerners are not "men like us". The difference is further explained when he says that they "took killing better than any natural men would ever do, and they had a way of yelling that didn't sound even partly human...without any brain behind it" (pp. 110-11). He confronts fear in war like Luther Dade and knows that it is going to change his life. He remembers what Sergeant Buterbaugh has said of the men walking away from battle; they are not "necessarily cowards", he says, but "just demoralized from losing their confidence" (p. 103). But Flickner knows that they are not just getting out of fighting, "they were trying to walk right out of the human race" (p. 114), he says. Away from the battle under the bluff, Flickner accepts his fear saying that he is not demoralized but scared. "I wasn't demoralized back there at the sunken road: I hadn't even lost confidence. I was just plain scared, as scared as a man can be, and that was why I walked away from the fight" (p. 120), he tells. In his outlook, Otto Flickner provides a contrast to the Southerners' stand on the past and even the twelve members of squad do the same.

The twelve Northerners of the squad belonging to the 23rd Indiana Infantry Regiment speak in monologues about their experiences in and what they think of war. The individual speakers are not always identified, but it is possible to discover their names in the monologues of the other squad members. The first member of the squad called Winter begins his narrative referring to history of his own. "Each of us had his history", he tells, "and each of the histories was filled with accidental happenings" (p. 163). His view of history as "accidental happenings" differs from that of Southerners' view of history as pattern. He is the only member to mention history and even in his case, he doesn't give much space to his past. The combined voices reveal the weariness of the battle the soldiers involved in field. The grim picture of the battle comes before us as one member of the squad, Amory witnesses the collective burial of the Southern soldiers. It makes him think that if the rebels' turn come, they will bury the Northerners in the same way. The last member of the squad, probably named Pope, can't understand their being at Shiloh. He thinks that the war is easier for the Confederates because they know what they are fighting for: independence and their land is being invaded. For the Northerners, he thinks, it is totally different; they are fighting because they are forced to fight. He also thinks that "it must be lots easier to fight *for* something than it was to fight against *something*" (p. 192).

The sense of history is involved with the action of the three white characters as they subject the blacks to fear and rage in *September September** (1977). The novelist Foote shows his interest in race relationships so that he accommodates both the black and white characters in this novel and confronts them with each other only to see the extent to which their relationship are conditioned by the past in the present of social upheaval—the Civil rights movement. The relationships

---

* Shelby Foote, *September September* (New York: Random House, 1977). All subsequent references in the text are to this edition.

between the two races in the South have been defined by the history; for the white Southerners the black, slave or free, have always been the means of achieving the leisure and enjoyment. The novel reveals that the past attitude of the whites towards the Negroes still governs the relationship between the two communities. The three white characters, Podjo Harris, Rufus Hutton and Reeny Perdew, kidnap a black boy of a wealthy family and ask a huge ransom for his release. The act of kidnapping, central to the novel, can be seen as the whites' retention of the past into the present; the black do exist for the sole purpose of gratifying the needs and desires of the whites. It is a historical crime committed by the white Southerners against the black Southerners. It has paralysed the whites for work and bring their fall; on the other side, it has made the blacks active for work and hence their rise. The novel shows that the black characters, Eben and Martha Kinship, have bright future; the white characters, who are paralysed by the past, do not have any future.

The white characters who are concerned with earning easy money use the racial crisis as the backdrop to exploit the blacks. The tension that builds among the races over the issue of the integration of Central High School in Little Rock provides them with right time for the crime. They know that the success of their plan of kidnapping depends upon the governor Orval Faubus creating the atmosphere of anger and fear. The governor has opposed the integration of the school thus has drawn the line between the two races. The chasm between the two races makes Rufus consider Memphis as the proper place for executing the plan of kidnapping. He knows that because of strong racial prejudice against the blacks there, the kidnapping of the nigger boy will slow down the police in investigation and it will more slow down the parents as far as their going to the law is concerned. Podjo, too, thinks that on the issue of the integration of the school, the church is with the white people. The white trio come to Memphis and their presence there is significant because, as in his earlier novel, Foote's fictional characters are involved in Major historical event. After the crime is done, the white trio attempt to pose themselves not as criminals but as Ku Kluxers joined hands with the Mafias in the Kidnapping. It shows how the whites retain the past for their selfish purpose.

For the black characters, Eben and Martha Kinship, victim's parents, the kidnapping of their son is an extension of the past system which has based on codes and tradition and governed the race relations in the South. Eben's first response to the kidnapping is to inform to the police but his father-in-law, Theo Wiggins stops him for doing it. "It's been a longtime rule of mine to stay clear of the law whenever and wherever the two colors involved" (p. 146), Theo tells. Theo knows that the law is whiteman's law and he sits on judgment on it. Eben is restricted to inaction and as a result he is overwhelmed with anger directed against the "System" which has controlled his life. But the system is faceless like the kidnapper so offers no target for Eben's rage. After a thought on the problem, he gives the system a face, i.e. the face of Theo Wiggins who has prospered by going along the system and becomes rich. Theo has used the whiteman's system against its creator for his own benefits. "It's a system that's been good to me. I used it against itself, and beat it" (p. 288), Theo tells Eben. For Eben, the system asks more without any reward from it; put and then take does not work in it. "For me", Eben tells, "the system was all put, with no take whatsoever except for wages from the job that was my reward for going along" (p. 241). It is the same system that prevents Eben from reporting the crime to the law. He rebels against Theo, the system, and gains a new life of independence. Eben has long hated the system even before he has married Martha, Theo's daughter. His rage that is directed toward the society "had been with him as far back as he could remember" (p. 217), the narrator tells.

Eben's rebellion against the system is his struggle to free himself from the history. He confronts the past in order to understand it. He sees the present event of integration of the school in the light of the past related to the Reconstruction following the Civil War. Eben knows that the Negroes will not get anything out of the present conflict as they did not get nothing from the Reconstruction. If Negroes have got anything, that is "trouble", "alienation" and "repression". The Reconstruction, as Eben sees it, has worsened the racial relationship in the South. In the time before the war, the Negroes had freedom and did get respect from the white masters that the outsider did not know. The black community which attempt to integrate the school will receive "the anger and enmity" (p. 19) of the white people in the region. Eben penetrates into the past and sees that the Negroes have started their struggle as losers; though they win, it will not matter anymore. Even Martha's response to the event surrounding the Little Rock School is conditioned by the past. Looking at the black mob on the television screen, she feels like the way "in the old days when a lynching came along" (p. 148). She recalls how they blamed the man who was cut and burnt for crossing the line of race. The victim was blamed because he proved the whites right in their view of the blacks as "animals out of Africa" (p. 148) by his own venture. The whites did exactly, Martha thinks, what they said they would do if the line of the race is crossed. Here Eben and Martha Kinship are stoical in their view of the past. The kidnapping makes the black characters to recall the past in order to review it; however, they gain from the event what the white characters lose.

The experience of kidnapping proves to be fruitful for Eben and Martha as they develop intimate relationship between them. Their new acquired intimacy is seen in their sexual response to each other. The sexual relationship between Eben and Martha before Teddy is taken is just a routine involving no exuberant response on Martha's part. After her short involvement with Snooker Martin, who helped her to discover her capacity for passion, Martha imposes a rigid self-control on her person after marriage. She undresses for bed, Eben observes, "without showing so much as an inch of flesh that had not been visible two minutes ago, when she was fully dressed" (p. 21). Martha attempts to suppress what lies in her blood that she calls the African past of "jungle doing". But under the pressures of the kidnapping of her son, Martha releases herself from this pattern. The night following Eben's slapping Martha in a fit of anger, both reconcile in the sexual act. There is urgency in the situation and the narrator describes that Martha "hitched up her nightgown herself, while he threw the bedclothes back, and in no time at all they were joined in a strain of mutual need" (p. 191). It contradicts their earlier experience before Teddy is taken by the kidnappers. Eben is seen lying across the bed away from Martha who "wrapped close as any mummy" (p. 21) and he is waiting "to get rid of what remained of the erection" (p. 22). As Teddy returns, their sexual experience becomes shared one and the narrator catches it in their conversation in the bed. At first, Eben complains but finds different response from Martha:

> "I ought to get some of this fat off.
> "I'll help you", Martha told him.
> "How?" He looked over at her.
> "You'll find out", she said (p. 284).

Both Martha and Eben laugh afterwards and the narrator describes them as the two happy people in Memphis. What the black characters gain, the white characters lose that all.

The relationships between the white characters become strained ones when Reeny Perdew leaves Rufus and moves to Podjo for her sexual need. Rufus's relations with Reeny reaches crisis as Teddy interrupts them in love-making that leaves Rufus "hanging". In order to master it, Rufus, who never drinks whiskey, empties a bottle of bourbon from Podjo's stock. When Reeny returns to the bed after putting Teddy back in the attic to resume what was interrupted, Rufus slaps Reeny in the face and in return Reeny, too, strikes him. Rufus's behavior towards Reeny on the occasion is strange because, Reeny tells, she has "come back down to get on with what we'd been interrupted in, both for his sake and my own, and there he was trying to maul me" (p. 172). Reeny is not only hurt but also left "hanging" so that she turns to Padjo for sexual gratification. Before kidnapping, sex for Rufus and Reeny was a matter beyond the realm of pleasure. They did find joy in each other and it is Rufus who undertook crime to support both of them.

The relations between Rufus and Reeny are based merely on sex and not on the code so they are broken when sex is not fulfilled. Rufus wants to keep Reeny because sex is the only concern in his life. When the object of his concern—sex with Reeny—is no more available or taken away from him, Rufus is broken within and loses control over himself that causes his death. Even the relations that builds between Reeny and Podjo have not grounded on history; their objective is sexual gratification. But in the bed, Reeny experiences a far different Podjo from the one she has expected. She hopes that Podjo will improve later and he, too, thinks that sex with Reeny will be better later. The novel reveals no future for the white characters since they end by their act; Rufus dies in the accident; Podjo and Reeny are seen reading ads in newspapers for job after Podjo loses all his dollars at the table in Las Vegas. The black characters learn from their past experiences but the white characters, on the other hand, are victims of the pasts—regional as well as personal.

Foote's characters both black and white bring their personal pasts into the present thus adding what Phillips, Jr., calls "shape and perspective to the presents".[3] They think about the past related to their childhood, youth and family. Their lives are so intricately involved with the pattern of the past events as they cannot free themselves from it. Rufus Hutton has a past which makes him what he is in the present. He follows the words spoken by his grandfather, Mr. Cilley who has worked in Lawrence Tilden's bank along with Harley Drew in *Love in a Dry Season*. In his death-bed, the old man tells Rufus, the young boy, not to trust the men who have the power and the means and he asks the boy to rob them at the same time. The old man has lived the life of honesty but now he realizes that it has been a mistake so that he asks Rufus to steal them in order to get justice. Rufus takes the advice of his grandfather to his heart and involves himself in a series of stealing the people. He begins from Ole Miss where he steals small thing that they call it 'pilfering'; it follows the theft in Marines and then burglary in the warehouse. By then, Rufus is so much used to the life of stealing and he conceives the idea of kidnapping and works it out with the help of Reeny and Podjo. Every time he is caught and punished; this time, too, he fails and loses Reeny for whom he planned the kidnapping. Rufus looks back at his past life, and sees a pattern of failure that governs it and extends into the present. Rufus's sense of the past governed by the pattern gives way to his sense of the region's history.

Rufus reads the books on history of Memphis, thus sharing Foote's interest in history. He knows that the present Leath school had been all white institution and was called Linden street school then. The knowledge of the past enables Rufus to see the change that swept over the region. There is regret in his voice when he says "Gone with the wind" (p. 5) as he watches the ruins of the old cabins while driving to Memphis. Rufus also knows a great deal about the history of English literature. He tells about his reading of Elizabethan drama, particularly, the *Duchess of Malfi*. He knows what Shakespeare might have felt when he completed *Macbeth* on the ground of what he himself felt after successful operation of the kidnapping. Rufus thinks himself as an artist who relies on lie for his creation. Podjo tells us that Rufus has created a make-believe life and he goes so far in that as he becomes a lie himself. For Rufus lie or pretension is, as Podjo thinks, the means to achieve his goal of manhood without any sacrifice. It is the Southern manhood that Rufus is after; the manhood of which Lee and Forrest are the epitome of. For the modern Southerner like Rufus, there is no other way to achieve manhood than through lie or pretension. Even sex with Reeny is a part of his goal and Reeny can see that Rufus is after more than merely sexual gratification. When Reeny leaves Rufus moving to Podjo, in a sense, she puts the question on Rufus's manhood that breaks his life.

Reeny's past which shapes her life offers the perspective to her present life. She inherits sexual freedom from her father-priest, Brother Jimson, who ran after the women whom he preached and the women "didn't mind sharing him any more than they minded sharing rain and sunlight" (p. 135), Reeny tells. Two men as husbands have come in her life before she falls in love with Rufus. Her second husband, Art Kinsella, has used her to please the men related to his dealing business and

Reeny slept with them for the sake of her husband and for herself, too. Her attachment with Rufus grows out of her lust and she follows him to the crime for money as well as for the sake of crime itself. Her life is full of repeated pattern of events extending into the present. Though Reeny lives with Podjo, she cannot forget the days she has spent with Rufus. She recalls how Rufus had brought her happiness in bed, on the seats of cars, in a phone booth and under the table. "You don't forget such things, such moments", Reeny tells, "all the balance of your life, wherever it takes you" (p. 174). The past matters to her but she knows that it is changed. "What mattered was what was between us, and what was between us now had changed" (p. 174), Reeny adds. The past is irresistible which comes to her with a force that may compel her to betray Podjo and go to Rufus again. She feels, the narrator describes, "a pang of sympathy for him, out of their old time" (p. 210) at Rufus's situation after she turns down his demand of sex. After his death in the accident, Reeny remembers his certain words he spoke to her in the past. The past wells up in her consciousness yet she lives with Podjo; it chases her in the present.

Podjo, too, brings his personal past into the present. He becomes one of many atheists of Patton's Third Army against the wish of his mother who wants her son to be a future priest. Free from the fear of God in the army, Podjo develops love for poker which later makes him a professional gambler. He runs after women when he retires from the army and in this period he kills a Buick dealer who sees Podjo in his place with his wife and tries to kill him with a butcher knife. After serving five years term in Parchman, Podjo comes out only to meet Rufus and follows him to Memphis for kidnapping. Podjo knows Rufus's grandfather who was a clerk in a bank but Rufus lies about him as a banker. The past is very much with Podjo; it is recalled by certain scene or things. On the way back to room after dropping Teddy, Podjo sees cotton wagon "creaking" on the road which reminds him of his father and his death. "I remembered my old man", he tells, "hauling logs that time of years, early fall...the day a chain snapped and the whole red-oak load came rolling down him" (p. 263). Podjo tells that his father, too, ran after women and admits that he has inherited that trait from his father. Podjo also knows Reeny as a school girl on the campus of Tarfeller School; he considers his own past and the past of Reeny as parts of the "wheel that came full circle" (p. 254). The personal pasts of the white trio throw light on their presents, thus help us to study them on certain ground. The same is the case with the black characters and their respective personal pasts.

The black characters, Eben and Martha Kinship have the sense of the past and time, and again they think of their pasts in the present. Eben Kinship tells his personal past which is significant in the making of his character. He has notion of the way of living that owes to the certain codes and thereby he tries to correct his sister's way of living which is nothing but sexual freedom. In the army, working with the black truckers, loaders and unloaders, Eben stays away from the white girls who praise the black on their faces. It is because, he knows that some day he will go home. His sense of place stops him from what the others do in the army. The past mode of living reflects on his present life with his wife, Martha. His loyalty to his wife is a matter of marvel for other women but to him it is buckling of principle and desire. "Women marveled at his fidelity to his wife", the narrator tells, "and it was true that he was faithful to her, both for her sake and his own, thereby linking principle and desire" (p. 13). After his marriage with Martha, his father-in-law, Theo imposes his own pattern on Eben's life. He reviews the past pattern in order to relieve it. Towards the end of the novel, Eben is free from all that Theo represents.

Eben's wife, Martha can see that her life is patterned after the plan of her father. In time of stress, Martha sees importance of the past in shaping the present. "What you have been makes you what you are, and in times of strain you see things in the pattern you never saw before" (p. 150), Martha tells. She attends Miss Endicott's Finishing School, to learn behavioral lessons because her father wants her to do so. She bids her time and keeps herself away from Negroes as her father has told her. Since her life is patterned by her father, Martha cannot know, even at the age of twenty-four, what to do when she meets young man like Snooker Martin. Her brief affair with him makes her aware of the thing which lies in her blood. She comes to know that in her blood lies "some wild animal" (p. 156) and that comes out as Snooker Martin beckons it. Martha's experience with him is beyond the pattern of her life, it goes back to the African past. "In my shame I decided what I felt went back to Africa, jungle doings" (p. 157), Martha tells. After her marriage, Martha takes care to rein up the animal lying in her blood. While she undresses for bed, she does not show even an inch of flesh of her body. She knows that the animal does not "rage" unless she lets it. It is her attempt to suppress her African past, but under the pressure of kidnapping, Martha changes and lets the African animal come out. Her letting the African animal out is an act of accepting the African past that she has been consciously suppressing.

NOTES

1. Robert L. Phillips, Jr., *Shelby Foote: Novelist and Historian* (Jackson and London: UP. of Mississippi, 1992), p. 56.
2. Phillips, Jr., p. 120.
3. Phillips, Jr. p. 218.

4

Narrative Technique

SECTION I: WALKER PERCY

The narrative technique that Percy uses in his six novels is highly ingenious in the field of novel writing. His main asset as a novelist lies in what Ashley Brown calls "his extraordinary observation of the social scene in the South".[1] He sees young men in the South suffering from a malaise in the midst of a postwar consumer society where appearance is everything. It reflects in his choice of his fictional protagonists, as a narrative strategy, who suffer from a malaise, a disease of which they have become acutely aware. In *The Moviegoer* Binx Bolling suffers from constant insomnia and shaking terror. Will Barrett of *The Last Gentleman* is given to fits of déjà vu and amnesia. The psychiatrist—hero of *Love in the Ruins*, Dr. Thomas More, has morning terror, disorientation and suicidal tendencies. Lance Lamar of *Lancelot* suffers from madness and kills his wife and her lovers. Will Barrett of *The Second Coming* sustains blackout and entertains suicidal tendencies too. Dr. Thomas More of *The Thanatos Syndrome* occasionally suffers from déjà vu. The malaise of these protagonists has to do with the presence they feel of the past in their lives. Percy uses the malaise as a metaphor implying the protagonist's preoccupation with his past.

Percy has special intention in using metaphor in his novels. Allen quotes from Percy's comments on the use of metaphors: "In his essay 'Metaphor as Mistake' Percy writes that all metaphors are literally nonsensical, but that out of their nonsense comes poetry, for in language, "beauty derives from ambiguity".[2] The metaphors enhance beauty of the novel while extending the central issues. The metaphor of 'malaise', of 'search' and of 'journey' do the same things in Percy's novels. Percy's fictional characters are often involved in a search. Their search consists of their attempts to discover into the past new clues of their lives, clues that will help to discover the future. It makes all Percy's fiction, what Hardy calls, "quest fiction".[3] The metaphor of search or quest is closely linked with the metaphor of journey. Commenting on the issue Mary Sweeny says that "In Percy's novels there is the feeling of a journey, of a progress, of his characters being in search of something."[4] The journey of the central characters is rendered in existential terms borrowed from the existentialist-philosopher Soren Kierkegaard. The use of existential terms such as "repetition" or "return" reveals character's preoccupation with the past. By using philosophical framework, according to Alan T. Belsches, Percy can help his reader "understand the importance of memory or a return to the past".[5]

The use of memory as a narrative device becomes obligatory on Percy's part since memory is a carrier of the past. The central characters are often visited by their past memories in Percy's novels. The memories are aroused in the central character's minds by the strategic device. "In a manner like Proust", Alan Belsches adds, "Percy uses sensory stimuli to arouse memories in his character's mind".[6] All the time the memories are closely related to certain places and time. The characters recall the memories of a certain time when they come to a certain place. The memories of the central characters are presented through the device of gradual recollection or flashback technique. In his four novels, Percy has made the central characters the narrators of the stories. The first-person-narrator-protagonists are given to brooding upon their personal and family history. It is so because they belong to the Southern community in which remembering is central act that Percy knows better. In this regard Alan Belsches writes that "the act of remembering remains central for his characters in the southern community".[7] As a result, the narrative that develops out of the first-person-narrator-hero's remembering becomes more reflective and distorted in sequence. Though

Percy uses the third person narration in two novels dealing with Will Barrett, he uses degrees of indirect discourse enough to identify the narration with their protagonists. There is no doubt that the first-person point of view is the most favored technique to Percy so that he begins a series of his novels with *The Moviegoer* having the first person point of view.

The text of *The Moviegoer** reveals its writer's skill in presenting the central issues through a technique that complies with it. He appropriately employs the first-person-narrator-hero, Binx Bolling, who is given to brooding upon his personal and family past making the novel first-person retrospect. In the opening first two pages of the novel, we learn a great deal about Binx's character and mentality. He is a freely self-revealing narrator. He begins the narrative in the present and in the following paragraphs, he treats us to reminiscences of his childhood as well as of the recent past. Binx tells, "This morning I got a note from my aunt asking me to come for lunch" and the next paragraph he begins with "I remember when my older brother Scott died of pneumonia" (p. 3). Using this technique Percy intends to show Binx's, what Hardy calls, "orientation to the past".[8] The past wells up in Binx's consciousness by force which result into his suffering from constant insomnia and shaking terror. Here insomnia is used as a metaphor in order to emphasize Binx's obsession with his family past. He is an insomniac for the family past visits him again and again.

Binx's past is tucked into the present narrative by using the cinematic technique of flashback which he knows better. The use of reminiscences or flashback is absolutely necessary in the given narrative, which covers only one week of hero's life, because we can learn more about his past through this technique. The past reminiscences entering the narrative make the book more episodic. In words of Jack Tharpe, "*The Moviegoer* is an episodic first-person recit by John Binkerson (Binx Bolling)".[9] Percy makes the novel episodic on a purpose.

* Walker Percy, *The Moviegoer* (New York: The Noonday Press, 1967). All subsequent references in the text are to this edition.

These fragmentary episodes reveal Binx's complicated consciousness. Commenting on this issue Lewis Lawson says that "these seemingly fragmentary episodes when pieced together, yield a clear picture of Binx's complicated consciousness"[10], Allen quotes. On the structural level these episodes are tied together with a metaphor of search. It is a sustaining metaphor used in the novel to describe Binx's preoccupation with his own past. Binx's search has many dimensions and one of them is father search. He searches into the past for the knowledge about his father. Percy describes Binx's search in existential terms borrowed from Soren Kierkegaard.

The existential terms of Kierkegaard form a matrix, a frame in which Percy conceives Binx's character. The existential terms used in the novel are not for what Kierkegaard thought of them but "what he (Binx) thinks and says they mean",[11] James Walter comments. In the light of existential philosophy, the search undertaken by Binx has two dimensions, "vertical" is the one and "horizontal" is the other. During his vertical search Binx has been preoccupied with the problems of time so that he reads great books, and particularly, books on history. Then he progresses to the horizontal search which involves such existential terms as "return" or "repetition" and "rotation". The term "return" implies a backward movement into the past in order to integrate one's past with the present. "This repetition ironically, includes the search for his father"[12], Jac Tharpe adds. Binx's act of moviegoing, an extended metaphor, far from being an escape, is one of the ways in which he conducts his horizontal search in time and space for clues. The movies become part of his search because he thinks they are onto search, they screw up his search. The metaphor of moviegoing is important because it stands for Binx and his world. "In *The Moviegoer*, the movies provide metaphors and similes for Binx and his world"[13], Pamela Freshney writes. It is in the movie theater that Binx first discovers place and time; the movies help him in finding genuine locality as they help him in his search.

Binx's search is sustained in the novel by the use of the metaphor of journey. Through journey, he can achieve "return" into the past. In this sense, his journey to his mother's fishing camp is his return into the past to know from his mother about his father. A "return" occurs as Binx learns from his mother that his father, too, pursued a search and that like his son, the father was a moviegoer. Here Binx's search for father fits the very terms "return" or "repetition". Similarly, Binx's train ride to Chicago with Kate and his bus ride back to New Orleans are journeys designed to illustrate his return to the past. His meeting with his old friend Harold in Chicago is not just a return to the past but it is reexperiencing the past as well. Percy's use of existential terms to describe the nature of his protagonist is appropriate because Binx feels alienated from his history and tradition of the South. He sees his alienation in terms of the alienation of the Jews. His alienation raises the question of his belonging, where does he belong? In order to find it out, Binx undertakes the search into the past contributing narrative progress.

The search of Binx, in other sense, adds the element of a detective story to the fictional narrative. He enjoys playing detective, finding more about his father. Like detective he holds proposition that there is something in the past that he needs to know. Percy devotes much of space in the novel to Binx's role as a detective. Making him act like a detective, Percy focuses on his protagonist's stance to the past. The other strategy of showing the central character's stance to the past is Binx's relation with his Aunt Emily. She is the past personified and her presence in the novel is the past moving around the protagonist. Carrier of the past values, she urges upon the capable Binx the performance of one's duty. To Emily the life of 'forms' or 'codes' is the only life that one can have. When she speaks, her speech is saturated with the language of 'forms' such as "grace", "honor", etc. Her ideal of human behavior is the Roman warrior Marcus Aurelias. Emily is the past stretching in the present therefore Binx's terms with her can be seen as his stance toward that past. Emily exercises her influence on Binx and it is clearly seen in his attempt to comply with the ideal behavior necessary for a gentleman. He becomes a soldier and goes to fight the Korean war. The aura of the past in the person of Emily clutches at Binx throughout the novel.

In *The Last Gentleman**, Percy adopts the narrative strategy different in several ways from its predecessor, *The Moviegoer*, to render the central issues. He shifts from the first-person-narrator of the earlier novel to an omniscient point of view of the third-person because *The Last Gentleman* has the protagonist who suffers from the illness of mind. The change in narrative strategy facilitates Percy to view his central character, Williston Bibb Barrett, from a distance as a sort of psychoanalytic case study. Barrett suffers from déjà vus and amnesia and this illness is the concern of the narrative. Amnesia is used as metaphor in order to describe Barrett's stance towards his personal as well as regional past. He experiences the attacks of compulsive memory from the past from which he wants to escape, and the particular form of amnesia offers him temporary relief from that memory. To Eric Jones the particular form of amnesia, which allows him to forget immediate past, "frees him from the responsibility of acting in accordance with his heritage".[14] Percy is so much concerned with Barrett's preoccupation with his past that he makes the novel's epigraph comment upon it.

The novel's epigraph from Kierkegaard's *Either/Or*, "If a man cannot forget, he will never amount to much" (p. 1), is appropriately quoted to signal Barrett's attempt to block from his memory the idea that he is the scion of a race now gone. The epigraph works as a preceding metaphor which directs to the novel's thrust. The action of the narrative springs from Barrett's attempts to escape from the haunting memory of the past, and his physically fleeing from the South to the North is a part of those attempts. Much of the narrative technique of the novel depends upon Percy's effective use of memory as a

---

* Walker Percy, *The Last Gentleman* (New York: Farrar, Straus and Giroux, 1966). All subsequent references in the text are to this edition.

carrier of the past into the present. Memory is used with its relation to the place where Barrett experiences that attacks of memory. He flees to the North because, as the narrator tells us, the South has places "redolent" with memory and he wants not to remember. The South is the place where Southerners experience history and this has to do with their sense of place. Even there in the North, Barrett's haunting sense of the past remains intact consequently the memory from the past wells up in his mind. Through the use of memory, Percy presents Barrett as a Southerner in whom history is internalized in the form of memory up to the mark where it assumes a psychopathetic quality. In words of Lewis Simpson, "In *The Last Gentleman* the internalization of southern history as memory in young Will Barrett assumes a psychopathetic quality".[15]

The use of memory requires a certain technique through which the event in the form of memory may be created. Percy employs the flashback technique to create the event that chases Barrett in the form of memory. It is through memory that Barrett's "return" to the past is achieved. A number of times he wants to return to the past in order to confront it and get relieved from it. But his final "return" to the past, through memory, does not occur until he physically confronts the place where the event of memory happened. As he stands before his father's house, Barrett is revisited by the memory prompted this time by the laughter of his aunts watching television on the porch. Thus Barrett's final "return" to the past through memory is made possible by his physical "return" to his father's house in the South. His physical return to the South is accomplished by using the metaphor of journey which is conceived as existential journey of the protagonist. It is a journey in search of roots to find meaning. Barrett's ailments are directly connected to his dislocations, his fleeing from the South, his lack of sense of place. Percy uses places in his novels, what Mark Johnson calls, "to represent the condition of the protagonist or of his society".[16] Ultimately, Barrett's search is a search for place where his father committed suicide.

Barrett's search for place involves his physical return to his father's house. Percy creates the Vaught family that makes

Barrett's return to the South possible by contracting him for its services. He fails to join that family at the appointed hour so he begins his journey to the South as he chases the Vaughts. He starts his journey from Manhatten through New Jersey into Levittown, then down South through Virginia tidewater, over to Alabama and Louisiana and thence through Texas to New Mexico. The novel becomes picaresque-episodic as Barrett visits strange people at strange place during his journey. Paul Gatson calls the book "a picaresque novel that can almost be plotted on a map".[17] The episodes are designed only to show the past's influence on Barrett. The episodes like Levittown and Forney Aiken, for example, are designed to reveal Barrett's obsession with his gentlemanly past. In those episodes, he acts like his father and grandfather did in a tight situation. Though the novel becomes more episodic, all those episodes are linked by the motif of return to his father's house. The motif is fulfilled when Barrett returns to his father's house and allows the memory to come. There is another motif used to map Barrett's preoccupation with the past, and that is motif of dance. It serves as an index of Barret's relation to his Southern past. Commenting on the issue Brian Flaherty says that "the dancing motif which runs throughout *The Last Gentleman* provides a fitting index of protagonist Will Barrett's nostalgic attachment to...his Southern heritages".[18] Living in an age of sexual license, Barrett looks back to an era of less social and moral ambivalence. He recalls how, even during the worst of the Civil War, Confederate officers attended balls and cotillions. Even he cites a letter from his forefather, an infantry colonel reading how he met Miss Sally Trumball last night. In fine, the dance motif reveals how Barrett thinks of the simple decorum of the Old South as a pure bliss.

In *Love in the Ruins**, Percy returns to the first-person-present narrative technique used earlier in *The Moviegoer*. Even the protagonist of the novel Dr. Thomas More claims to

---

* Walker Percy, *Love in the Ruins* (New York: Farrar, Straus and Giroux, 1971). All subsequent references in the text are to this edition.

have similarities with his predecessors in the matter of mental problems. More too suffers from an illness of depression and morning terror. He tells of himself, "I am subject to attacks of elation and depression, as well as occasional seizures of morning terror" (p. 11). His mental sickness has to do with his personal past and works as an extended metaphor in the narrative. More has a traumatic past revealed through the conventional flashback technique which is fairly necessary in this narrative covering only four days in his life. Percy begins the action of the novel in the present, has his hero become unconscious, then flashes back to the past before returning to the present at the novel's end. Since in the flashback technique everything is recollected, Percy uses a device of gradual recollection for that. This technique helps Percy in extending the narrative beyond its temporal limit. The narrative becomes more distorted in sequence as More recollects the pieces from his past life. This distortion is deliberate since Percy presents through it, what Hardy calls, "a naively inverted historicist mentality".[19] More opens his narrative in the present and then goes back to the past related to his beloved daughter Samantha's death and his wife Doris's running away with a heathen Englishman.

The reality of Samantha's death from the disease neuroblastoma is unbearable to More consequently he develops depression and morning terror. More tells, "My daughter died, my wife ran off with a heathen Englishman, and I fell prey to bouts of depression and morning terror" (p. 20). His times with his daughter that he describes as "The best of times" (p. 12) ends with her death leaving him alone in a role of mythmaking. As a result More sees American history and his past in mythic terms. He heightens his own past into a particular myth of death and loss. He sees Lola, one of his girls, in terms of the Southern agrarian myth; to him she represents *Gone with the Wind*. He thinks the present times in terms of myth of apocalypse used as a pervasive metaphor in the narrative of the novel. This metaphor is introduced very early at the opening page of the novel. "Here I sit, in any case, against a young pine, broken out in hives and waiting for the end of the world" (p. 13). The subtitle of the novel, *The Adventures of a Bad Catholic at a Time Near the End of the World* involves the metaphor of apocalypse.

The apocalypse is a metaphor of More's vision of the world which encompasses the narrative structure of the novel. His description of signs of apocalypse begins with "The center did not hold" (p. 18) an allusion to Yeats's poem "The Second Coming"[20], describing the end of the present civilization. More has already experienced the end of the world in the death of his beloved daughter, and this traumatic past gives way to his apocalyptic vision. He projects his interior apocalypse on to the external world. Percy uses similes and symbols in order to describe the approaching end of the world. As he observes the surrounding, he sees obvious signs of disorder. The interstate slab is cracked, vines are sprouting from it; poison ivy has captured the speakers posts at the local drive-in-movie; cars are left rusting in parking lot. There are clashes between black and white; the parties are politically polarized, and the Church is divided, too. These signs for More furnish a tangible evidence of cultural disintegration. The violence of imagery, plot and narrative voice make the novel powerfully apocalyptic. The end of the world foreseen by the protagonist is the end of the world in his consciousness. So, the metaphor of apocalypse is one that explores the mind of More.

The other metaphor used in the narrative is the metaphor of search. More's quest for harmony in the chaotic world is designed to show his orientation to the past. One of the dimensions of his quest is theological—he is longing for the world of innocence and bliss as is suggested in the word lapsometer. It is a device for measuring lapes and is designed to diagnose a kind of "second fall" which modern man suffered. More renews his efforts to restore mankind to a primal Eden through his invention. Ideally, this lapsometer will lead man back to paradise; it will allow man to reconcile body and spirit, control love and hate, anxiety and ennui, depression and exaltation. More's quest for harmony carries him into the diverse areas of science, religion and history. He feels drawn also to the Middle Ages and the unclouded moral certainty of his namesake, Sir Thomas More, who likewise dreamed of utopian existence. During his search, More reads books on history in order to find out the roots of the present apocalypse. He learns from his study that apocalypse is a historical process and cannot be stopped. His search is conceived in existential terms. Percy embeds the existential idea in the narrative in order to tell the importance of "return" to the past for the protagonist.

More thinks him a wayfarer like Robinson Crusoe and travels through four-zoned world of Fedville, the swamp, town and Paradise Estate—"an ironic symbol of human longing for prelapsarian happiness"[21], Kennedy comments. His "return" to the prelapsarian happiness is made possible by the creation of Art Immelman's character. Being evil himself, Art plans to use the lapsometer for evil purpose of creating anarchy in society. In his attempts to foil Art's evil plan, More prays to his historical namesake, Sir Thomas More. His prayer is a sign of his "return" to the old faith because towards the end of the novel, More is seen enjoying a Christmas Eve with his new family.

Linda Hobson uses the terms "first-person confession of a madman"[22] to describe the narrative technique of *Lancelot**. The term is appropriately used because the text is an outcome of the facts of the protagonist, John Percival. The use of confessional mode, as part of narrative strategy, suits to the narrative whose protagonist-cum-narrator is burdened with the past and tries to unburden it by confessing it to the other. The protagonist Lancelot's confession takes the form of a long and very personal monologue as the listener John Percival keeps quiet during its course except on the last two pages of the novel does he speak in monosyllabic words "Yes" and "No" (pp. 256-57). Except for Percival's responses, everything in this novel according to Hardy belongs to, "the form of the dramatic monologue".[23] Basically dramatic monologue is a technique used to reveal the character of a person speaking it.

---

* Walker Percy, *Lancelot* (New York: Farrar, 1977). All subsequent references in the text are to this edition.

Allowing Lancelot to speak monologue, Percy leaves the reader to see the mind of the protagonist. Lancelot's entire monologue is a meditation of his own past. It reveals him as a Southerner preoccupied with his aristocratic lineage. His is a mind closed within history as is suggested by the use of setting. Percy makes Lancelot speak from a solitary cell in a Center for Aberrent Behavior symbolizing Lancelot's living in a world of the past not shared by the others. The locale of the novel brings one of the central metaphors into focus. It is a place where Lancelot is undergoing treatment for illness of his mind called madness.

The metaphor of madness unfolds Lancelot's mind fully preoccupied with the heroic ideals of his family past. Trying to live by those ideals, he kills his infidel wife and her lover and then sets the Belle Isle on fire. By society's standard, the act of Lancelot is the act of a madman and his romantic obsession with the past ideals is a form of madness. The voice we hear in the novel is the voice of a madman confessing what he has done. Linda Hobson's comment on the nature of Lancelot is worth to quote here. She says, "As the narrator or confessor... Lancelot is truly mad, has been made so by trying to live by stoical, ethical values in an aesthetical, relativistic society".[24] Being mad himself, Lancelot faces difficulties in remembering the past. However, to him those difficulties are due to the banality of the past, and he sees the past intolerable. The narrative that comes up from him is in the form of fragmentation. The development of the narrative largely depends upon Lancelot's remembering and structuring the past into an ordered form. The narrative becomes fragmentary as he recollects the pieces from the past and puts them down into a sequence. "Like a man assembling a jigsaw puzzle", Dowie comments, "Lancelot picks up and puts down the pieces of his past, trying to construct the fragmentary into a whole".[26] Since the act of remembering is central in the narrative, the protagonist relies heavily upon memory.

Percy uses memory as a narrative device which flashbacks in Lancelot's mind the past that he wants to reconstruct. While reconstructing it, he sees his wife's adultery in relation to his childhood experiences of his father's corruption and his mother's possible affair with Uncle Harry. The acts of remembering and organizing the past become for Lancelot the means of coming to grips with the banal and intolerable past. It is a way to restore himself to some sort of sanity. Although he declares the past as banal, he knows that it contains the clue to the present and needs to be searched. Lancelot's search is designed only to show the extent to which he is obsessed with the heroic ideals of the past. His search, though negative one is born of his daughter's blood type "O" which is the proof that he is not her father. The whole novel is built around Lancelot's discovery that Siobhan cannot be his daughter because of her incompatible blood type. He begins his search to find out when his daughter was conceived and where he and his wife were at that time. His obsession with the blood relationships is his attempts to live like his ancestors. In words of Allen, "In his desperate attempts to identify with his antebellum ancestors, he exhibits an intensely southern obsession with blood relationship."[26] His search is divided into two phases: one stretching up to killing of Margot and burning the house afterwards; second leading to find clues into the past.

The first phase of Lancelot's search is intended to see sin and it directs the development of the novel. Percy patterns the search on the Holy Grail quest described in the medieval Arthurian legend. There is a corresponding thread between the action of the novel and the medieval quest. Brinkmeyer, Jr., points out the similarities between Lancelot's quest and the ancient one. He says, "Percy strikes corresponding chords between the action of the novel and the medieval legend of the quest for the Holy Grail".[28] However, Percy twists his protagonist's search making it for unholy grail—to see sin in his wife's bed. Still Percy intends to tell here that these two quests—Ancient and the modern—are meant to revive the heroic act. Nourished on the heroic ideals of the South, Lancelot sees his wife's infidelity a cause enough to perform the heroic act. The code of chivalry demands decisive action only after the truth of the event is revealed. In order to find the truth of his wife's infidelity, Lancelot searches the documents, receipts and bills of the past that show Margot's absence in the house during the period the daughter was conceived. Once it is made clear then Lancelot's search is directed to find out the daughter's real father. He plays as a detective working on his case very meticulously. Like in his earlier novels, Percy uses the elements of detective story both for thematic and structural purpose.

Lancelot's single-minded detective-like pursuit leads him to employ Elgin, his black servant, to spy on his wife. He asks Elgin to prepare videotape of the activities that will happen in Margot's room. Any step taken to save honor is justified, even asking the servant to peep into his wife's bedroom. Lancelot's search which is originated from his obsession with the heroic ideals, leads him to kill his wife Margot and her lover. The act of Lancelot's killing his wife can be seen as an act of revenge. Seen from this perspective, the story of the novel becomes a tale of brutal revenge of a husband on his wife. This element of revenge tale, too, presents Lancelot as a Southerner preoccupied with the code of honor. Killing his wife and burning the house mark the end of the first phase of his search. The second phase of Lancelot's search begins in a cell of a New Orleans asylum where he is admitted, after the Belle Isle incident, for his insanity.

The second phase of Lancelot's search is born out of his immediate need of organizing the fragmentary past. He has to remember the past though banal and intolerable in order to give it a form or shape. His search, through remembering and organizing the past, is the only means to come to terms with the past. As a result, the narrative becomes an absolute recollection of the past events. In Lancelot's search, Percival is an important figure because it is he who screws up his search into the past. Or, rather Percival is a listener to the confessions of a madman. Percival's time-to-time visit to the cell encourages the patient to speak uninterruptedly since Percival keeps dumb. The quest convinces Lancelot that the present age is the age of paltriness and should be rejected. Dismayed of the present age, Lancelot wants to build a new society in that old womblike seat of Southern glory and defeat, the Shenandoah Valley. The new society as Lancelot conceives will be based on the codes of courtesy and chivalry by which the noble men of the past acted. Lancelot's conception of a new society strongly reveals his obsession with the Southern past. Although Lancelot's search has two phases, the search as a unique metaphor underlines the theme and helps to develop the plot of the novel too.

*The Second Coming** as a sequel to *The Last Gentleman* does share its predecessor's narrative technique to a large extent. Both novels have the same protagonist and they are told from the third-person point of view instead of more intimate first-person point of view of the other novels. Using self-conscious omniscient third-person narrator, Percy attempts to give a mere detached portrait of a Southern hero trying to come to terms with his own past. The protagonist Williston Bibb Barrett in his mid-forties has changed considerably in the past twenty years, particularly his amnesia condition has taken a complete reversal. Now in this novel, he suffers from a total recall, the intrusion in his mind of incidents from the past. It is the memory of the incidents related to his father does visit Barrett again. That he is visited by his father's memory is implied in the title of the novel. Commenting on it Allen says, "This novel is...*The Second Coming* of the ghost of his father."[28] The title itself is used as a metaphor to describe the condition of the protagonist. This total recall of the memory from the past is a sickness; it is a sickness of consciousness used again as an another metaphor in the narrative.

The sickness of Barrett has been emphasized at the outset of the novel. The text opens with Barrett on the golf course suffering from disorientation and falling down. He is overcome with the memory, as he goes to retrieve the golf ball, of a time when his father had tried to kill him on a hunting trip to Georgia when he was a boy. Though Barrett does not willingly set out to recall the past, rather the past by way of memory overtakes him many times in the course of the novel. Here

---

* Walker Percy, *The Second Coming* (New York: Farrar, Straus and Girour, 1980). All subsequent reference in the text are to this edition.

memory is used as a strategic device to show the past's major influence on character's life. Closely associated with this device of memory is the device of sensory stimuli. "Percy uses sensory stimuli to arouse memories in his character's mind,"[29] Belsches remarks. At the beginning of the novel, for example, the sound of the fence wire stretching and the sight of hawk recall to the hunting incident in Barrett's mind. These two narrative devices contribute to rendering the central issues in the novel. Throughout the narrative the memory of the past is stimulated in the Barrett's mind and it is in the memory he tries to search meaning. Since Barrett's search for meaning dominates the narrative, Percy uses the search as a metaphor to convey the protagonist's stance toward the past.

Thus Barrett, though outwardly changed to some extent, is still a searcher for meaning. Not only the thematic development but also the narrative development of the novel depends on Barrett's search. In this regard Allen has to say that Barrett is an "anxiety-ridden searcher" and "the progress of the novel is his retracting of his life in order to find the point at which it all went wrong."[30] Once again Percy describes his protagonist's search on existential line providing what Alan Belsches calls "a philosophical framework that can help his readers understand the importance of memory or a "return" to the past",[31] Though the literal "return" does not occur in the novel, the protagonist returns to the past with the help of memory. Using the technique of flashback memory, Percy recreates events from the past which are important to Barrett and those he wants to understand. One of them which is prime important to him is the hunting event. It is "Only one event that had happened to him in his life. Everything else that had happened afterwards was non-event", the narrator tells (p. 52). The piecemeal return of the memory of this event occurs all through the novel while Barrett searches meaning in it. Before the final return of the memory occurs, Barrett descends, as a part of his searching, into a cave.

The dark cave into which Barrett descends symbolizes his mind obsessed with the dark past of his father's death. His wandering in the cave conveys his attempts to understand his dark past. At the same time the one-eyed mountain on which Barrett lives takes on a brooding presence, "symbolizing his father and his father's suicide",[32] Sweeny remarks. Likewise Percy uses the symbol of place in order to exploit his protagonist's sense of place which underlines the sense of the history too. In words of Jac Tharpe, "any mention either of time and place is automatically a part of the symbolism of time-place".[33] Thus Barrett's sense of the past is inherent in his sense of place. His speculations on time and place begins quite early in the novel. His problem is associated with time and place. "Will has the essential problem with time and place",[34] Tharpe adds. Throughout the novel the memory associated with certain time and place chases Barrett. The time is the past when his father killed himself and the place is near Thomasville, Georgia where the event happened. In order to block out the memory of time and place, Barrett fantasizes having sex with Ethel Rosenblum on a nondescript plot of land near the railroad station in Ithaca on the way of his father's funeral. His fantasizing sex is a defense he creates to block the memory of time and place. However, it is significant to note that Barrett gets relieved from this memory of time and place when he confronts it in a hotel. Thus using symbols of places Percy focuses on the central issues.

In addition to these symbols and metaphors discussed so far, Percy uses another metaphor to convey Barrett's problem with the past. That one is the metaphor of apocalypse. This metaphor comes into play early in the novel as he becomes convinced that all the Jews have returned to Israel which he takes as a sign that second coming of Christ is near. Barrett's brooding over the apocalypse is a strategy that he has developed in order to escape his father's death. Even Allen remarks that Barrett's musings over apocalypse are his "efforts to work out through the trauma of his father's death".[35] The traumatic experience of his father's suicide is taken in by Barrett in terms of apocalypse which is reflected even in the title of the novel. *The Second Coming* refers, first, to the second coming of Christ and the destruction of the world and next to the second coming of his father in the form of memory.

Though he has developed the apocalyptic musings as a strategy to block the irresistible memory, it does come rushing back into his mind as his apocalyptic musings intensify. Thus apocalyptic musings are not the proper alternatives to the memory; that one is present in the person of Allison.

The narrative of Allison is incorporated in the novel's text for thematic purpose. Percy designs three narrative sequences: the first centers on Barrett, the second on Allison and the third on Barrett-Allison engagement with one another. In the first seven chapters Percy alternates between Barrett's narrative and Allison's narrative. This alternating scheme of narrative suggests the oscillation of Barrett's mind between the past and the future represented by his dead father and Allison Huger respectively. Symbolically, Barrett's oscillation is between "Thanatos" and "Eros"[36] and he has to choose one. Here Percy provides a cure for Barrett's sickness; the cure lies in Eros represented by Allison. Barrett has to accept the past and build future with Allison. Her character is complementary to Barrett's: he remembers everything; she is clean of memory; he falls, she raises. The love story of Barrett and Allison, which forms the third part of the narrative, suggests that the process of Barrett's illness has started. Creating Allison's character without memory, Percy means to say that history is a matter of remembrance for those who have memory.

*The Thanatos Syndrome** has the narrative technique more or less similar to its predecessors, yet distinctive in some respects so to be evaluated on its own terms. Percy reintroduces Dr. Thomas More as the protagonist and chief spokesman in this novel. In order to focus on his protagonist's stance towards history, Percy recreates a quasi-mythical territory, the "Feliciana" country. In italicized preface, Percy tells about it emphasizing its distinctiveness among industrial pollution. It is a microcosm of the Old South. Its way of life-plantation life, bourbon served in Jefferson cups, early morning

---

* Walker Percy, *The Thanatos Syndrome* (New York: Farrar, Straus and Giroux, 1987). All subsequent references in the text are to this edition.

fishing—is similar to the way of life of the Old South. Tom More belongs to such a place. His belonging to "Feliciana" moulds his character and also gives him enormous advantage over his enemies. As a part of his narrative strategy, Percy's creation of mythic place serves as locale of the novel and a setting against which we can judge Tom More's character. He acts in accordance with the way of life of Feliciana—like a gentleman throughout the novel. Unlike the other protagonists of Percy's novels, Tom More is least mentally ill. He is shown as a keen observer of the happenings around him.

At the outset of the novel he tells, "For some time now I have noticed that something strange is occurring in our region" (p. 3). To him little things are more important. What he observes is that there are personality changes in several of his patients, including even his own wife. Tom More's attempts of unraveling the mystery covers the largest space of the novel. Its progress in a sense depends upon Tom More's penetrating into the possible cause of the changes in his patients' behavior. The pattern of the mystery story is exploited here in order to reveal the protagonist's approach to the past. In mystery story the protagonist does solve the puzzle piece by piece and he is able to penetrate into each character's mind that the reader cannot. The upper hand is given to the protagonist as he must come to the truth of mystery. At the same time, in mystery story the event is happened in the past and the detective has to begin his search in the present leading to solve the mystery related to the past. So having chosen the first-person point of view, Percy "gains much by that choice",[37] Hobson remarks. Tom More as scientist-detective learns at a pace and keeps the novel in progress. His search is the main concern of the narrative.

Tom More's search is born out of his curiosity and his concern for his fellow humans. The metaphor of search, the most favored to Percy, is developed here in order to underscore Tom More's genuine sense of the Southern past. Like Binx of *The Moviegoer*, Tom More's search has two dimensions: horizontal and vertical. However, his search is free from any philosophy, from debts to Kierkegaard or Dostoevski. His horizontal search includes journey from place to place offering his reflections on the past life of the people of the South. The metaphor of search is interlinked with the metaphor of journey which, to some extent, brings about Tom More's return to the past. His visit to Lucy's plantation house can be seen as his return to the past. The plantation house symbolizes the Old South and its owner Lucy is the chatelaine of that house. Tom More's journey to the fire tower of Father Smith has both thematic and structural significance. He visits the priest who has climbed up into a fire tower in order to escape the trouble of the world and that visit marks his vertical journey. There on the tower Father Smith confesses to Tom More his past related to his inclination to join the Nazis. The confession of Father Smith runs several pages of the novel under the caption "Father Smith's Confession" (p. 239). It is an attempt on the part of the priest to come to terms with his own past and, at the same time to warn Tom More on the basis of his knowledge of the past. He conveys Tom More that social engineering by Comeaux and his lot is a very much similar to Hitler's genetic engineering team for improving the Aryan race. Father Smith's confession is a powerful narrative within the main narrative that screws up Tom More's search.

What Tom More is searching for is clearly stood out in the title of the novel. The title means "the symptoms producing death". Tom More's search for symptoms which produce death implies the Southerner's love of death. Percy's structural strategy is primarily based upon his use of search as an extended metaphor. It joins both the main plot concerning Tom More's unraveling the mystery about his patients' behavior and the sub-plot consisting of Father Smith's confession together. Having received clue from the priest, Tom More reaches to the root of the mystery. He comes to know that Bob Comeaux and his group of doctors are adding heavy sodium to the local water supply to engineer a New Eden. On closer inspection, Tom More realizes that Comeaux is fooling people under the name of restoration of a mythical past. His genuine sense of the past, revealed through the metaphor of search, helps him to see Comeaux's conspiracy wrapped under the cover of restoration of the past. As a Southern gentleman of "Feliciana", Tom More foils Comeaux's attempt and acts 'noblesse oblige' towards the common people saving them from danger.

The narrative technique, to sum up, of this novel differs from the earlier one in that here plot is made more important than character. As a result, the narrative that we see is more straight and easy to read. Though the protagonist is past oriented, there is no flashback memory. Commenting on the technique of the novel Hobson says, "Since plot is more important than character here, the narrative pushes straight through time and easy to read, with few flashbacks".[38] But it is the novel in which Percy creates setting sharing with the narrative technique of Shelby Foote.

SECTION II: SHELBY FOOTE

The narrative technique in the novels of Shelby Foote is compatible with the central issues that he deals with. His novels are carefully designed and meticulously constructed leaving the impression of highly crafted artifacts. His narrative technique, primarily, consists of creation of setting—time and place—which gives validity to the central issues. As a novelist-historian, Foote is very particular in the historical accuracy of the setting of his novels. "The historical accuracy of the setting for his fiction has been important to Foote from the beginning of his career",[39] Robert Phillips comments. Foote's novels are located either in Jordan County, Mississippi, or Bristol whose past and tradition the characters cannot escape. In creating an imaginary locale to his novels, Foote owes a great deal to Faulkner. In this matter Robert Phillips has to say that in writing novels Foote cannot escape the influence of Faulkner.[40] Like Faulkner's Yoknapatawpha, Foote creates new terrain for his novels. The creation of place has to do with the past of it. That is why Foote recapitulates the past of a particular place going as far back as to its origin. The importance of place in Southern culture is due to the history of the region. History gives meaning to place. The Civil War, according to Robert Phillips, is "an immense event that gave the place a new meaning for all time".[41]

The characters in Foote's novels have sense of place; they "belong" to certain place. Their's abandoning the "place" symbolizes their's drifting away from the moorings of the past and tradition. In a sense, the place in Foote's novels serves as microcosm of the South; its history is the history of the South. As for the creation of time in Foote's novels, it is inherent in creation of place. In addition to the history of the place, Foote clearly establishes "historical milieu"[42] for his works. *Tournament* is based on the life of Foote's grandfather and develops around events that led up to and included 1910, "a sort of watershed year."[43] *Follow Me Down* is based on the sensational murder committed by Floyd Myers in Greenville in 1940 and the trial that followed in 1941. The depression year provide a backdrop for the events in *Love in a Dry Season.* The battle at Shiloh during the Civil War is the subject of the novel *Shiloh. September September* takes place in the month of September in 1957, another of those "watershed" years,[44] Foote calls it. Thus Foote's novels are set in the recent past which serves as the backdrop against which the action of his novels develops. In words of Thomas Landess who says that history is used as "the matrix in which the central action takes place".[45] In such setting, Foote develops his fictional characters.

Foote uses the dramatic technique of characterization which makes his novels the novels of character study. The story is developed mainly through, what Louis D. Rubin, Jr. calls, "the dramatic and psychological exploration of the interaction of his characters within a known historical context".[46] Foote delineates his fictional characters in a tragic perspective. The fortunes of the characters are described in terms of their rise and fall, and their fall is necessarily due to the flaw in their characters. The characters's preoccupation with the past turns out to be the flaw causing their fall. Foote's treatment of the characters is more symbolic; they represent the Southern community and their fall implies the fall of that community. Foote achieves the effective characterization through the use of wide range of narrative technique—from the first-person monologue through the third person narrator to the multiple points of view. Usually the first-person monologues are the memories from the past that come to the character preoccupied with the past. Here Foote employs the flashback technique which makes the return of character's memory possible. He also uses multiple points of view only to offer different perspectives to characters or event thus helping readers to see truth. Most of the time Foote builds his characterization with the help of an extended metaphor or motif which communicates the central issues in the novels. On the basis of the comments so far, we can assume that, Foote's narrative technique consists of creation of time and place, psychological exploration of characters, and use of different monologues. Through the effective use of this narrative technique, Foote extends the central issues of history and individual consciousness in his novels.

The narrative technique used in *Tournament** merges and coincides with the central issues. Foote's choice of the third person omniscient point of view is appropriate because the novel intends the objective study of the protagonist Hugh Bart. The third person narrator is no other than Asa, the grandson of Hugh Bart. Asa undertakes a kind of search to learn about his grandfather from the people intimately related to Bart. At the opening of *Tournament*, Asa tells that "talking to others who knew Bart while he came and strove and went, that I learned the full story" (p. xxx). Asa, as the narrator, devises the life-story of Hugh Bart in terms of rise and fall of his character beginning with his coming to Lake Jordan during a late-Reconstruction at the age of eighteen; his becoming sheriff of Issawamba County at twenty-two; his becoming owner of Solitaire plantation; his marriage with Florence Jameson and afterwards having children from her, and Asa ends with Bart's selling the land only for his destruction and death. In view of Thomas Landess the action of the novel "is primarily concerned with the rise and fall of the heroic Hugh Bart."[47]

---

* Shelby Foote, *Tournament* 2nd edition (Birmingham, Alabama: Summa Publication, 1987). All subsequent references in the text are to this edition.

Foote employs the elements of tragedy, what Asa call "the decline and fall" (p. xxix), in order to emphasize the tragic aspect of Bart's character in a given time and place.

The time created is the past surrounding the Civil War and its aftermath, and the place is the plantation Solitaire on the periphery of mythic Jordan County. Foote devotes an ample space to the origins of the plantation itself and to the character of Isaac Jameson, who first carved a cotton empire out of the wilderness and lived to see that empire and house destroyed by the Northern invaders. Here Foote does not intend to write a novel about history "Yet history is the matrix in which, the central action takes place, and Foote carefully constructs his enveloping action in order to emphasize the historical dimensions of his major character"[48], Thomas Landess comments. In such a time and place, Bart undertakes stewardship of the land and his act can be viewed as the "historical equivalent" of the Southerner's efforts to "come again" after the ravages of the War and Reconstruction.[49] With consistent efforts, Bart rises to power of sheriff but declines and falls from that height due to his obsession with the region's 'style'.

Foote creates Bart as a Southerner who carries with him certain traits which lead him to imbibe the 'style'. Billy Boy, the long-time servant to Bart views him as "the proud tall figure cast his shadow, immense and knightly and biblical rich, unreal glare of hero-worship" (p. xxix). That Bart's obsession with the 'style', which creates barriers enclosing him and causing his fall is explicitly projected in the novel's texture by the use of the extended metaphor of enclosure. "The growth of the barriers that enclose is one of the central metaphors through which Asa explores Bart's fall; the other metaphor is the tournament, the game"[50], Robert Phillips comments. The metaphor of enclosure comes into play when Bart thinks manners as important as goal. While describing Bart's attempt towards maintaining manners Asa says that "The minute he found himself thus, coat spread open, belly shoved forward, he would know that he had dropped what he believed was his air of gentility, and he would snap shut like a turtle jerking back into its carapace" (p. 19). The manner or 'style' becomes for Bart a shell, carapace in which he encloses himself.

The 'style' of "grand life" proves too constricted for a man like Bart. He does not understand that men admire him not because of his superficial style but because of his person. Instead of going beyond the superficial style he prefers to live within it. The style creates barriers that thicken around him. It stops him from doing action like the one that he has started stewardship with. Asa tells us that "he had begun to put on weight, flesh building a barrier about the robust frame, incasing the still-hot blood", and, Asa continues he "took sanctuary within inaction" (p. 53). Like the region's 'style', tournaments too encloses Bart leaving him inactive.

Bart's obsession with tournaments, games is put in a clear perspective by Robert Phillips. He says that "Bart's games are described in terms that are often associated with American and European culture in general, but specially with the South".[51] The European writer Walter Scott romantically glorified games as crucible from which heroes emerge. And the Southerners took Walter Scott too much seriously, and Bart is no exception to it. Bart loves the game of hunting up to the level where it becomes obsession to him. He likes "the acrid smell of powder blown back across his face, the feather explosion of birds in midair" (p. 35). When there is less plentiful hunting in the Delta, Bart turns to trapshooting and then ultimately to poker. He does extremely well in these games and emerges as a champion. But these games create barriers around him and because of that, Judge Wiltner says, he "stopped changing" (p. 52). The games that enclose him, draw him away from his family and become the source of his isolation from it. Bart filled Solitaire with trophies, but the cost he pays for being often away from it is that "he hardly knew any of his children" (p. 132). Consequently the children fail to live by the pattern that he imposes upon them.

The metaphor of enclosure is also reflected in the form of the novel. Asa's narrative surrounds and encloses the story of Hugh Bart. The opening and closing comments by Asa are set apart on pages numbered in Roman numerals enclosing pages of the central narrative of Bart. Further, his enclosure in the past is suggested again by the same metaphor, this time implicit in the plantation house where he does live. The forty-room mansion which he restores to its past glory closes him both what Phillips calls "physically and spiritually".[52] The Solitaire represents the past and its restoration implies living the past in the present. Living too much past in the present becomes the means of Bart's defeat.

Bart's obsession with the past and his attempt to recount it towards the end of the novel, is conveyed through an appropriate method. The method Foote uses is the episodic structure since Bart sees his life history in terms of individual episodes/incidents. All of them are as Bart sees it very much important to him for they have touched his own life in one way or the other. Asa tells that how Bart think "All the lives that had touched his own, some of them only slightly, had a share in the telling. Cass Tarfeller, Abe Wisten, Major Dubose: all these were a part of his life" (p. 223). The problem Bart faces here is that he can't tell all those episodes since it would require as much time as has been required to live. Yet he can't omit one of them because it would leave a space blank on a canvas bigger than life. Bart tries to search an essence, a string that would bind those individual episodes touching Bart's life and binds them artistically in a metaphor. Every episode or incident related to Bart reveals that all the time the persons involved in it tried to live by the pattern of the Old South. Cass Tarfeller episode, for instance, shows Tarfeller living by the code of chivalry forced upon him. The episodic structure suits to the novel as it extends Bart's stance towards history.

The narrative technique of *Follow Me Down** is similar to that of *Tournament* and *Shiloh* in many respects. All of three novels have the contrasting narrative voices and a framing device for their action. In this novel, Foote retains the technique of creation of time and place for handling the central issues. The story of the novel develops in a cultural context and

---

* Shelby Foote, *Follow Me Down* (New York: Random House, 1978). All subsequent references in the text are to this edition.

place that the characters exemplify. Foote deliberately recaps some of the background of Solitaire and Jordan County, where the main characters of the novel live, "in order to make certain that the reader understands the extent to which his characters are exemplary of their own time and place",[53] Landess comments. The narrative focus of the novel is on Luther Eustis's preoccupation with the traditional faith that leads him to murder Beulah. So making him the inhabitant of the Solitaire, Foote has emphasized what Landess calls "the orthodox nature of the world"[54] exercising its influence on its inhabitants. Thus Eustis's obsession with the traditional faith is in keeping with his being an inhabitant of Solitaire, the symbol of traditional society. To emphasize the orthodox faith of Eustis further, Foote uses the Bible as a frame of reference. Eustis is dominated by a desire to follow the letter of the Holy Word, and throughout the novel, he refers to the Bible as he faces crisis. Eustis represents "the intrinsically protestant morality"[55] providing a base for nineteenth century conservatism of the region.

Creation of time and place shows Eustis's orientation to the past. Creation of other characters also delineates Eustis as a man who was led to the traditional faith. One of those characters is Brother Jimson, the old-fashioned preacher who picks up the young sinner and dashes him against a tree, the action exemplifying his nature. Jimson's religion relies upon emotional extravagance and being one from Jimson's flock Eustis follows it. The other character created for the purpose is Beulah. She represents loose morals, a trait associated with change from old to new. The creation of Beulah's character has thematic importance since she challenges the traditional faith of Brother Jimson. A part of Foote's narrative strategy involve in his pushing Eustis between the old faith and new force represented by Brother Jimson and Beulah respectively. Foote knows that what a person like Eustis will do when he finds himself between the two extreme poles. At first he is attracted to Beulah, runs with her to an island where he has had sexual relations with her. Eustis, however, as he is obsessed with the protestant morality, feels guilty and begins to hear voices commanding to kill Beulah. Killing of the girl is the central act in the narrative leaving ground for assessment of the central issues in the novel. After the killing of Beulah the novel is molded upon the story of crime and retribution—an extended metaphor again through which Foote communicates society's views upon Eustis's obsession with the past. Foote appropriately employs a multiple points of view representing the voices of community.

The technique of multiple points of view allows many characters to comment on the central event helping reader reach to its heart. Foote says that the purpose of notion of employing nine narrators "was to penetrate to the heart of an event".[56] In a sense it is a way of interpreting past event from different perspectives. Each of the narrators views Eustis's past action in a certain context. Among the narrators Ben Rand, the circuit clerk, who opens the novel introducing us to the principal characters and gives the general outline of the plot leading up to the verdict. Mildly cynical and humorous point of view, Ben gives Bristol's general views. To Ben the middle-aged Eustis does not look like a man who could "entice a girl into a soda shop" (p. 9). Roscoe Jeffcoat, the jailor closes the narrative and like Ben Rand represents the community's view. Roscoe is not as cynical as Ben and has sympathy for Eustis.

Russell Stevenson and Parker Nowell occupy the second level of narration. Quoting Foote's comment Phillips says that both are "more involved and closer to the action".[57] They offer a more complex perspective because of their learning and experience. With these two things they measure the significance of the events and their own relationship to it. Stevenson's narrative gives picture of a world with no fixed vision. His world is populated with references to the past, allusions to important cultural and historic events. He seems not to care about Eustis. Yet Milton's fallen angel comes to his mind as he recalls his first visit to Eustis in the jail. Events surrounding the murder of Beulah remind him of passages from Shakespeare and Milton. He knows the story of the Bible-reading Eustis; knows something of the history of Jordan County and looks for the Old South under the concrete facade of the New. These references offer a framework, Phillips says, "against which the reader may judge Eustis".[58] We can see the historical dimensions of Eustis's character but Stevenson doesn't care. Stevenson is, Parker Nowell observes, "hard faced already from living off the misdeeds of the people" (p. 220).

Nowell Parker, Eustis's lawyer narrates two sections balancing that of Stevenson. He is a disillusioned and frustrated man enjoying intellectual status and knowing the ills of the modern world. Keats, Browing, Chaucer, Emerson and especially Shakespeare constitute a portion of Nowell's literary background which provides him with a frame of artistic and historical reference in which he can see and judge the present. For example, the tale of Eustis's wife, Kate reminds him of Troilus and Cressida and of Emerson. "What she told me had occurred in an atmospheres much like that of *Troilus and Cressida* in which the faithful are betrayed and the brave are slain. I was reminded of Emerson's 'Our faith comes in moments; our vice is habitual,' Parker tells" (p. 219). Forms and patterns constantly affect Nowell and he is consciously using his understanding of form to shape his case to its best advantage. As he knows the facts, he thinks that he can shape the case to fit almost any pattern the jury may seem to want. Making the case simple is his duty, complications will loose the case. Parker thinks Eustis's crime in terms of failure of love which is traceable to events surrounding the Civil War. He sees the South's defeat in the Civil War as the root cause of the present illness of the society including the illness of Eustis.

We are made known of Eustis's past through the technique of flashback memory used in Kate's, Eustis's wife, narrative. She traces the roots of her husband's crime in his family heritage. She tells that Eustis inherits in his person the double heritage of lust from his mother and murder from his father. To Kate the past bears on Eustis's present. The narratives of Eustis and Beulah form the middle of the novel. Eustis narrates six sections that surround a single central section by Beulah. In his narrative he tells how he sees Beulah, and attracted to her; takes her to the island and kills her there. His narrative delineates him as Bible reader following instruction from God.

He is not satisfied with the present world; Bristol to him is like a concrete wasteland. Beulah's narrative occupies the center of the novel and takes place as Eustis drowns her. At the center of her narrative is the long seven-page summary of the important events of her life touching her meeting Eustis. The narrative of both Eustis and Beulah recall the past into the present focusing on the narrative thrust of the book.

*Love in a Dry Season** has the technique which corresponds to the central issues treated in it. As usual, Foote renders the central issues through the technique of creation of time and place and through effective characterization. The novel is set in Bristol, the county seat of Jordan County at the time of depression years and the period surrounding the World War Second. This immediate historical setting becomes more prominent in the novel. Against such setting, Foote develops the characters who are not away from it. To be objective in character development, he employs the third person point of view. The use of flashback technique which facilitates the writer not only in telling more about a character or event but also suggesting the character's orientation to the past. Foote begins near the end of an event and he immediately reverts to earlier events that preceded and then finally adding a sentence to the culmination of the event. Following the same technique, Foote opens novel with the announcement that "Major Malcolm Barcroft was sixty-seven when he died, the last male of his line" (p. 3) and then for the next twenty-five pages, Foote surveys the history of the Barcrofts and their position in Bristol. In the same narrative fashion, we learn about other characters in the novel—Harley Drew, and Amy and Jeff Carruthers.

The flashback technique thus enables the reader to learn more about the past of the character which is outside the plot of the novel. The qualified third-person omniscience examines the feelings and ideas of the major characters penetrating into their, what Phillips calls, "troubled consciousness."[59] Malcolm

---

* Shelby Foote, *Love in a Dry Season* (New York: Random House, 1979). All subsequent references in the text are to this edition.

Barcroft has that troubled consciousness and the narrator explains it in relation with the events surrounding the Civil War. Malcolm Barcroft's intense preoccupation with the Civil War is the point of emphasis in the Barcrofts narrative. He plays the battle in his mind; the Civil War internalized in him. It is shown in Malcolm Barcroft's playing a crate of lead soldiers while demonstrating to his only son the mechanics of the Fredericksburg's battle. His reverence for the military tradition and the frustration that followed after he is denied opportunities to comply with that tradition leaves him insensitive to his children. As a result, Malcolm Barcroft is isolated from his daughters and that isolation results into the 'failure of relationship'. It fails due to the lackness of love which in turn doesn't grow in a dry season. The 'failure of relationship' serves as a unified metaphor along with 'the metaphor of dry season' uniting the two contrasting plots; the Barcroft's plot and the Carruther's plot.

The Barcroft's plot is developed on the failure of father-daughter relationship. Frustrated as he is Malcolm Barcroft hasn't any attachment towards his motherless daughters. He fills their breasts not with fatherly love but with anger and reproach. His behavior to his daughters is like a stern soldier commanding discipline to his subordinates. He doesn't like Florence's pretense of suffering from hot due to her long yellow hair, so that he arranges his regular barber to cut it. She cannot bear the shock she received during her hair cutting which visits her in dreams in the form of her father sexually assaulting her. Malcolm Barcroft's manners to his younger daughter Amanda, too, lacks fatherly love. He refuses Harley Drew's proposal of marriage with Amanda on the ground that Drew can not remember the color of Amanda's eyes. After that the lovers—Amanda and Drew—plan elopement but Malcolm Barcroft senses it and threatens to disinherit Amanda. Malcolm Barcroft never means that Amanda should not marry; she must marry a person he chooses. He invites Henry Stubblefield, ex-soldier to court Amanda but she rejects him. The father-daughters relationship are failed because Malcolm Barcroft lives by the military code that he tries to impose it on his daughters. The father-daughter relationship is doomed to fail since it is not based on love. On the other side, the relationship between lovers—Amanda and Drew—is failed because it is not based on true affection, true love on the part of Harley Drew. He is not so much after Amanda's love as he is after her father's fortune. Harley Drew breaks his relationship with Amanda as he sees great prospects in Jeff's wife, Amy Carruther.

The metaphor of failure of relationship dominates the Carruther's plot. The father-daughter relationship is at failure in the Barcroft plot due to Malcolm Barcroft's preoccupation with history embodied in the Southern military tradition. Ironically the relationship between Amy and Jeff Carruther fails because their sensibilities lost their moorings in history. Their marital relationship is an utter failure since their marriage is not based on a deep affection for each other. Foote develops their characters metaphorically. Jeff is a voyeur, and even, as Amy suggests, a homosexual and to the other end Amy is promiscuous. Jeff has no sensibility for history and Amy, though she inherits Briartree, misses the fundamental of the tradition of which Briartree is a symbol. Amy and Jeff restore the plantation house but they are not "Old Miss" and "Mars Jeff" in the old sense of the words. Their lives are not those of planters although they move into the plantation house. Without moorings in history and tradition the lives of Amy and Jeff become increasingly violent. It is explicitly shown in certain events such as Jeff's motor accident making him blind, his killing the pet dog; his shooting at a man in Amy's bedroom in a hotel near Nice; his attempt to kill Drew, and finally his smashing the face of Amy, his wife. In their failed relations, the central metaphor works; it works at three levels of relationship: father-daughters, husband-wife and lover-beloved. These relationships are failed because the season is too dry for the growth of love which can sustain them.

The 'dry season' mentioned in the novel's title is employed as an extended metaphor in order to bring the central issue into focus. The metaphor of dry season provides the novel with a context in which its action takes place. Actually depression years are the time in which the novel is set. Foote metaphorically looks at those years as the season which is dry in the sense that it lacks manners, rites and tradition all forming the conditions of love. Love cannot grow outside these conditions consequently the human relationships which need love are failed. The relationships between Malcolm Barcroft and his daughters, between Amanda and Drew and between Amy and Jeff are devoid of love, hence doomed to fail. The metaphor of the failure of relationship springs from and merges into the metaphor of dry season. It shows Foote's skill in extending the central issue in an appropriate technique.

The narrative technique in *Shiloh** is appropriately used in order to bring the central issues into light. The major ingredients of Foote's narrative technique are the creation of time and place and subsequent development of characters in that setting. Here Foote recreates the battle of Shiloh, one of the crucial encounters in the Civil War through a series of monologues by people engaged on the Southern side and the Northern side. The battle is appropriately recreated through a series of monologues in order to examine the Southern mind in relation with history. The battle is viewed through the eyes of five soldiers, Union and Confederate, and a squad of Indiana men. Foote alternates the Southern soldiers' monologues with the Northern soldiers' ones. This technique of alternation helps the writer present the Southern mind in comparison with its Northern counterpart in the context of the Civil War history. The battle of Shiloh provides Foote with an occasion to bring the Southern and Northern people face to face in the crucial moments of history. In this light, the battle proves to be a 'pervasive metaphor' serving the thematic purpose of the novel. The metaphor facilitates us to see comparatively the 'difference' in characters of Southern men and Northern men extending other metaphor, the metaphor of difference.

Southern narrators and Southern interest do dominate the novel *Shiloh*. Palmer Metcalfe, Lieutenant on the Southern

---

* Shelby Foote, *Shiloh* (New York: The Dial Press, 1952). All subsequent references in the text are to this edition.

side, narrates both the opening and closing sections of the book. The Southern narrators employ many more pages in which to explain their presence. This makes the book the Southern novel. It takes its stand, what Phillips calls "in the interest of the Southern cause and Southern history" and the Northerners provide a "counterpoint" representing an industrial and mechanical force.[60] In a sense, the Southerners differ from their fellow Northerners in terms of their way of life, and more importantly, in their sense of the past. The narrative of the novel which springs from the 'metaphor of the battle' focuses on the difference in character of the Southern soldiers and the Northern soldiers, and in understanding that difference lies the understanding of the central issues. The difference is achieved through creation of Southerners as more "reflective" than their Northern counterparts. The Southerners are reflective because, Phillips says, "they have...a more significant past on which to reflect".[61] All the Southern narrators, Metcalfe, Luther Dade and Sergeant Polly, reflect on the past. The Southerners, as Metcalfe's father asserted, are in love with the past. Metcalfe's narrative, crucial in thematic sense, is full of references to his past life.

Metcalfe, during the course of his narratives, reflects on his own past. He recalls the words of Sherman about the defeat of the South spoken at the Louisiana Military Academy where Sherman was superintendent and Metcalfe was a student. He dips even further into his past as he sees images of his mother, whom he knows from painting, floating into his consciousness during sleep. Johnston's death gives Metcalfe yet another occasion to reflect on what his father had told him about the South's malady which caused the region's fall. Metcalfe recollects his father's words, "We were sick from an old malady, he said: incurable romanticism and misplaced chivalry, too much Walter Scott and Dumas read too seriously" (p. 200). This is not all; Metcalfe does reflect on a European past too. For that purpose he is deliberately placed by the author at the center of strategic planning of the battle which facilitates him to comment on South's obsession with the European past. Metcalfe admits that the fault lies in

Southerners' patterning the Shiloh battle order on Napoleon's Waterloo battle order. The South's obsession with the European past not only leads it to the war but also leads it to defeat. The South's attachment to a European past is further revealed in Metcalfe's quoting lines from Keats and Shakespeare. It gives his prose poetic quality.

On the other side, the Yankees do not quote Keats or Shakespeare, and Flickner would like to forget about Napoleon. Flickner's father told Flickner stories of his grandfather's having fought against Napoleon, but to Flickner tales of past seemed out of place. He thinks that their country is new country and they do not need stories from the past. Among the Federals only Flickner comments on the past but it is only to deny it. The Northerners have nothing to do with the past, the Southerners, on the other hand, love to remember the past.

The further difference between these contrasting people lies in the fact that the Southerners appear in the form of community that their counterparts lack. In the course of their narratives, the Southerners mention their meeting each other that gives their tale an internal coherence. The Southern army seems to be more of an organic whole as Luther Dade appears in each narrative of his fellow Southerners. More, the Southern men have much closer ties with their officers whom they serve. Metcalfe's father was close to Johnston enough to serve as a second for Johnston in a duel. The Southerners form a community which is closely tied together. Sergeant Polly's relationship with Forrest is very close and Polly is under his direct command. The closer ties of the Southerners are counter pointed against the more distant ties of the Northerners. Fountain is not as close to Grant as the Southerners are to their officers. He knows about Grant because both have come from the same section of Ohio State. One reason that Southerners' ties stand out more clearly, Phillips tells, is that "the past has deeper meaning for the Southerners. Their past is more closely connected to who and what they are".[62] To sum up the artistic use of the technique consisting of the creation of setting and use of metaphor of battle and metaphor of difference helps the reader to understand the central issues in the novel.

September September, the last novel, claims to have the similar technique that Foote has employed in his earlier novels in order to extend the central issues. His strategy of developing the story in a historic context is naturally used here. He sets the novel in the month of September 1957, a time of the Civil Rights Movement giving way to the local racial conflict over integration of a school in Memphis, the novel's locale. The events happening around the month of September 1957 are special to Foote because he sees them "in terms of the nation's history, particularly in terms of the Civil War history", Phillips comments.[63] In such time and place Foote develops his fictional characters who alike their creator are not far removed from major historical events. Foote brings four of his fictional characters from Bristol to Memphis, and three others from Moscow, Tennessee, to Memphis. Foote uses the racial conflict as a backdrop against which events in the novel take place. This backdrop has been sustained throughout the novel by the use of news media. Headlines from the papers create that backdrop as the characters read them.

Foote creates two sets of characters, one white, one black matching thematically. His choice of the characters from both races is a part of technique adopted to examine the black-white relationship in historical context. The relationship between the two races is conditioned by the history and when they are juxtaposed, they play history. These two races are confronted in their historical roles—exploiter and exploited—as the white characters kidnap the only son of a wealthy black family for a huge ransom. The event of kidnapping implies the white men's attempt to retain the past into the present. The event provides the black people with an occasion to review the past in order to build a new future. In the narrative structure of the novel, the kidnapping is a crucial event used as a metaphor extending the central issues. Another metaphor used is the metaphor of conflict: it works in conflict between two sets of characters as well as in conflict within two set themselves. For Phillips the conflict within two sets themselves are more significant "in the thematic development of the novel".[64] The event of kidnapping puts unusual pressures upon the internal relationship within the characters. Under the pressures, the white characters break one from other and left to their loss; the black characters come more closer and are at their gain.

The black characters' gain and the white characters' loss are presented in terms of success and failure of their sexual relationships. The crisis in the relationships between Reeny and Rufus occurs when Teddy, the kidnapped boy, interrupts their lovemaking. Reeny turns to Podjo for her sexual need after Rufus beats her and leaves her hanging. Before kidnapping the sexual relationships between Reeny and Rufus were exuberant, binding them closely together. Podjo is not as good in his sexual relationships with Reeny as she imagined him before she leaves Rufus. As their relationships fail, the white characters experience death and dissolution towards the end of the novel. Rufus is killed in his Thunderbird accident; Podjo and Reeny are off to Las Vegas where Podjo loses thousand dollars. Through the metaphor of kidnapping, Foote explicitly tells that the white characters are bound to fall because they try to live by the past sucking the blood of the blacks. The metaphor of kidnapping gives way to the metaphor of conflict which brings about the fall of the white characters. The black characters, on the other hand, gain much out of their experience. They develop a much closer sexual relationships contrasting to the earlier ones, before kidnapping, which were just meaningless gratification. After their son, Teddy returns home, Martha and Eben develop a less restrained, more exuberant shared sexual relationships. For Eben, it is emblematic of his achieved manhood and escape from the system of the unwritten codes governing race relations. Foote's populating the novel with both black and white characters is as much part of his narrative technique as creating metaphors.

Foote delineates his fictional characters in two ways; one, what the general narrator tells about them in the four sections of narrative allotted to him, and other, what the characters themselves think in their monologues. The general narrator presents every character commenting on him or her and on occasion, he tells us what the community thinks about him or her. The characters' monologues are divided into three sections labeled as "Voices". It is a narrative device that Foote uses in order to give a room for characters to reflect on their various pasts. This device suits to the central issues of the novel because the "Voices" of the characters are the voices of individual consciousness reflecting on its past. Having caught in the current events, the characters in the novel bring a considerable portion of their own pasts to these events so that, Phillips comments, "the past adds shape and perspective to the present". They reflect on their pasts while identifying it as the sole determinant of their present being. Thus Rufus tells how his present life has to do with his grandfather's advice to steal the rich people in order to take revenge on them on the old man's behalf. Podjo recalls his military career which has shaped his present making him a professional gambler. Reeny thinks her past life has made her what she is in the present. Like these white characters, the black characters, too, think of their past to understand the present.

Among the black characters, Martha sees her present life from the perspective of the past. Under the pressures of kidnapping, she explores the old foundations of lovemaking journey back to the primitive origin of love "jungle doing", she calls it. Eben, too, adds his own past to the present while thinking the kidnapping as an extension of the slavery system. Eben thinks of Theo, his father-in-law as the intricate part of the system. Foote's creation of Theo's character is thematically important because Theo lives by the system which emasculates Eben. Eben's conflict with Theo, after the kidnapping event, is naturally with the system itself. It is that system—the unwritten codes and traditions—which has governed race relations in the South. Eben rebels against Theo and his system since they are the root of his present problem. Eben's rebellion against the system and his rejection of it is symbolic. His rejection of the system is his rejection of the past. But he does so only after he understands it.

NOTES

1. Ashley Brown, "Walker Percy: The Novelist as Moralist", *Walker Percy: Novelist and Philosopher*, eds. Jan Nordby Gretlund and Karl-Henz Westap (Jackson and London: UP. of Mississippi, 1991), p. 169.
2. William Rodney Allen, *Walker Percy: A Southern Wayfarer* (Jackson and London: UP. of Mississippi, 1986), p. 143.
3. John Edward Hardy, "Man, Beast and Others in Walker Percy", *Walker Percy: Novelist and Philosopher*, p. 144.
4. Mary K. Sweeny, *Walker Percy and the Postmodern World* (Chicago: Loyola UP., 1987), p. 1.
5. Alan T. Belsches, "Life over Death: The Use of Memory in Walker Percy's *The Second Coming*", *Southern Quarterly* XXIII-4 (Spring, 1985), p. 37.
6. ——, p. 40.
7. Belsches, p. 37.
8. John Edward Hardy, "Percy and Place: Some Beginnings and Ending", *Southern Quarterly* XVIII-3 (Spring, 1980), p. 5.
9. Jack Tharpe, *Walker Percy* (Boston: University of Southern Mississippi Twayne Publisher, 1983), p. 46.
10. Allen, p. 22.
11. Jame Walter, "Spinning and Spieling: A Trick and a Kick in Walker Percy's *The Moviegoer*", *Southern Review 16.3* (July 1980), p. 576.
12. Tharpe, p. 62.
13. Pamela Freshney, "*The Moviegoer* and *Lancelot*: The Movies as Literary Symbol", *The Southern Review* XVIII-4 (October 1982), p. 727.
14. Eric L. Jones, "Percy's Parousia", *Southern Quarterly* XXIII-4 (Spring, 1985), p. 50.
15. Lewis P. Simpson, "The Southern Aesthetic of Memory", *Tulane Studies In English* 23 (1978), p. 223.
16. Mark Johnson, "The Search for Place in Walker Percy's Novels", *Southern Literary Journal* VIII-1 (Fall, 1975), p. 76.
17. Paul L. Gatson, "The Revelation of Walker Percy", *Colorado Quarterly* XX-4 (Spring, 1972), p. 469.

18. Brian P. Flaherty, "Walker Percy's *The Last Gentleman:* An Invitation to the Dance", *Notes on Mississippi Writers* XIX-1 (1987), p. 1.
19. Hardy, p. 13.
20. W.B. Yeats, *The Second Coming*, *W.B. Yeats: Selected Poetry*, Ed. Timothy Webb (London: Clays Ltd., St Ives PIC, 1991), p. 124.
21. J. Gerald Kennedy, "The Sundered Self and the Riven World: *Love in the Ruins*", *Art of Walker Percy: Stratagem for Being,* ed. Panthea Reid Broughton (Baton Rouge and London: Louisiana State UP., 1979), p. 124.
22. Linda Whitney Hobson, *Understanding Walker Percy* (Columbia, South Carolina: University of South Carolina, 1988), p. 93.
23. John Edward Hardy, *The Fiction of Walker Percy* (Urbana and Chicago: University of Illinois Press, 1987), p. 140.
24. Hobson, p. 97.
25. William J. Dowie, "Lancelot and the Search for Sin", *The Art of Walker Percy: Stratagem for Being,* p. 245.
26. Allen, p. 123.
27. Robert H. Binkmeyer, Jr., "Percy's Bludgeon: Message and Narrative Strategy", *Southern Quarterly* XVII-3 (Spring, 1980), p. 88.
28. Allen, p. 132.
29. Belsches, p. 40.
30. Allen, p. 132.
31. Belsches, p. 37.
32. Sweeny, p. 54.
33. Tharpe, p. 113.
34. ——, p. 114.
35. Allen, pp. 132-33.
36. ——, p. 137.
37. Hobson, p. 148.
38. ——, p. 151.
39. Robert L. Phillips, Jr., *Shelby Foote: Novelist and Historian* (Jackson and London: UP. of Mississippi, 1992), p. 29.
40. Phillips, Jr., p. 37.

41. Phillips, Jr., p. 38.
42. ——, p. 29.
43. ——, p. 29.
44. ——, p. 29.
45. Thomas H. Landess, "Southern History and Manhood: Major Themes in the Works of Shelby Foote", *Mississippi Quarterly* XXIV-4 (Fall, 1971), p. 325.
46. Louis D. Rubin, Jr., Foreword, "Asa Bart's Way", *Tournament* by Shelby Foote (Birmingham, Alabama: 1987), p. VIII.
47. Landess, p. 324.
48. ——, p. 325.
49. ——, p. 324.
50. Phillips, Jr., p. 55.
51. ——, Jr., p. 56.
52. ——, Jr., p. 166.
53. Landess, pp. 325-26.
54. ——, p. 327.
55. ——, p. 326.
56. Phillips, Jr., p. 91.
57. ——, p. 94.
58. ——, p. 96.
59. ——, p. 114.
60. ——, p. 76.
61. ——, p. 77.
62. ——, p. 78.
63. ——, p. 28.
64. ——, p. 218.

5

Conclusion

The study of the works of both Walker Percy and Shelby Foote in the preceding chapters reveals the central concern of these two contemporary writers of the South. They are concerned, no doubt, with the question how the Southern characters respond to their past while living in the present. In the fictional worlds created by these two writers, the history of the South exercises its control over the lives of fictitious characters. In the novels of Walker Percy the central characters are preoccupied with the personal, or the family past which is inevitably and inextricably related to the past of the South. They are subjected to the burden of the past. They try to bear the past's burden, try to comply with the past, but fail in their enterprise. However, their preoccupation with the past continues unabated making them restless in the present. This is what happens to Binx Bolling of *The Moviegoer* who is obsessed with the heroic tradition of his family past. Binx tries to follow that tradition, becomes a soldier that representing the standard of character appropriate to the son of a Southern gentleman under the circumstance. Even after having become soldier, Binx fails to keep himself with the family tradition because he does not meet hero's death in the war. However, the heroic spirit, though consciously and subconsciously repressed, continues to live deep in his psyche. His sense of failure to live up to the family tradition and his obsession with the heroic ideals make him restless in the present.

Like Binx, Will Barrett of *The Last Gentleman* is the scion of an old Southern family carrying the burden of following the model of behavior of an old style gentleman like his great-grandfather. But the initial ability of the ancestor to act with assurance has declined into uncertainty of his son and irony of his grandson, Will's father, who in a moment of despair shot himself. Will's bonds with the gentlemanly past impels him to ponder on the Civil War history but his father's ironic death due to the gentlemanly past leaves him confused and anxious. Not the gentlemanly past like Binx and Will but the past related to the death of his beloved daughter and wife is a burden heavy enough to bear for Dr. Tom More of *Love in the Ruins*. The past of loss of the beloveds is constantly in his mind putting him in the role of mythmaker. No matter how Dr. More may mythologize the past, the past haunts him and keeps him from participating fully in the present. As the scion of a Southern aristocratic family, Lancelot Lamar of *Lancelot* bears the burden of his family heritage constituted of a series of great deeds. He is a hero with a repressed need for performing something profound and courageous. While he rejects the past as banal, he never really gives up the dreams of heroic ideals. In his new colony in Virginia, he decides to revive the lost code of honor and female virtue. As Lancelot does his best to break away from the Southern past, the more he is bound to it.

The reappearance of Will Barrett in *The Second Coming* shows him increasingly obsessed with his past related to his father's attempt to kill his son and later on his killing of himself. Will's obsession with the past has to do with his attempt to know what actually happened in the past. The past of his father's suicide is so unbearable to Will as it impels him to flee to the North. However, there in the North, too, the past haunts him. Like Will Barrett the memory of his father haunts Dr. Tom More of *The Thanatos Syndrome*. But he is less preoccupied with his personal past and more with the Stedmann history. His obsession with the Stedmann history generates in him the sense of ending, of apocalypse. He imposes the myth of apocalypse on the modern situation. There is no break in his obsession with the Stedmann history even after he is on spree along with his new family.

The characters' mere obsession with the past to Percy is an illness related to the mind. It is implied in the characters' suffering from the diseases concerned to the mind and called by various names in the novels. In *The Moviegoer* Binx Bolling suffers from constant insomnia and shaking terror. His illness is related to his failure in living up to the heroic tradition of his family past. His sense of failure gives way to his sense of alienation from the tradition affecting his natural gifts, sleep. Another character from the novel Kate, Binx's love, has psychiatric symptoms such as anxiety and suicidal tendencies. Kate's emotional disturbance is in a large part engendered by the pressures of her parents who want her to be a sweet and docile Southern belle of the past. So that Kate's illness is born out of her resistance to the forced conformity to the past rather than out of her obsession with the past. In either cases the characters suffer from the illness of mind. Will Barrett of *The Last Gentleman* is given to fits of déjà vu and amnesia. He sleeps poorly, often forgets to eat, suffers from headaches and finds himself in disorienting fugue states in which everything looks strange. To cope with his illness, he is undergoing psychotherapy. Will's sickness has to do with the tremendous influence on him of his family heritage. Unable to comply with it, he develops the illness of amnesia which blocks from his memory the idea that he is the scion of race now gone and thus frees him from the responsibility of acting in accordance with his heritage.

The heavy drinking psychiatrist, Dr. Tom More of *Love in the Ruins* suffers from "mourning terror", disorientation, and suicidal tendencies. He is declared crazy, hospitalized and kept under lock and key for a good long time. More's sickness is inextricably related to the past that wells up in his consciousness. The loss of his only daughter and wife is a burden heavy enough to bear for More that leaves him to heavy drinking. At the same time he is prone to romantic mythologizing which is a sickness common in Southern men revealing their inability to confront the present in a positive manner. Lancelot Lamar of *Lancelot* is declared mad and put in the Centre for Aberrant Behavior, New Orleans where he is undergoing treatment for his mental illness. Lancelot is obsessed with the history as a series of great deeds and laments for the lost possibility of heroic action which he believes existed in his fore-fathers. His laments takes the form of a romantic obsession with the heroic action that leads him to murder his wife and so by society's standard, he is mad. He needs psychotherapy and his reconstructing the past can be seen as his going through an apparently one-sided psychotherapy. His monologues are instrumental in restoring some sort of sanity in him.

Will Barrett of *The Second Coming* suffers from the total recall—the intrusion on his consciousness of the past memory that makes it impossible for him to live in the present. He also sustains blackouts and entertains suicidal tendencies. Considering all this, Will's sickness is the sickness of consciousness resulted from his intensive obsession with the past related to his father's suicide. The disease contaminates Will's present life and abnegates the possibility of his having future. The other character Allison Huger, Will's love, too, suffers from mental disease, that is, amnesia. She, according to her doctor, is psychotic. She has been admitted in the Valleyhead Sanitarious where she is subjected to electroshock therapy which has left her with almost no memory. But Allison's amnesia is not so much the result of the electroshock as it is the burden of the past. If Allison cannot remember anything, or has hard time remembering, it is not because for her there is nothing to remember, but because the past memories are too painful to tolerate. Living with amnesia, Allison uses notebook as a guide to the past. Dr. Tom More of *The Thanatos Syndrome* though apparently seems to be least mentally ill of all the Percy heroes, suffers from the disease of obsession with the history. He is obsessed with the Stedmann history which generates in him the sense of ending. He imposes the myth of apocalypse on the present situation. His predilection for myths is the part of illness, the part of defense to face the present.

Dr. Tom More's appearance in *Love in the Ruins* and his reappearance in *The Thanatos Syndrome* show him a man given to mythmaking that he never frees from. He is the embodiment of the Southern character having the habit of distortion and romantic mythologizing. Similarly, Father Smith's sickness, his fascination with Germany, is the sickness of the Southern character since fascination with Germany has indeed long been a part of Southern mind.

Percy's proposition is that the characters' sickness of mind leads to a rather empty life. They escape the present and least think of the future since they are preoccupied with the past. Their problems are that they cannot simply forget the past and get relieved from it. For that matter the characters in Percy's novels take stock of the past implied in search into the past to make the present living condition. Once the characters understand the past, they are exorcized of it, or pattern their lives upon it. Binx Bolling of *The Moviegoer* does the same; he searches into the past for clues to his father's predicament in relation to his family's heroic ideals. He tries to learn more about his father from 'his own mother'. It is his "return" to the past in order to understand it. Binx learns that his father was suffering from personal gloom born of English romanticism that killed him. This knowledge about the past, about his father helps Binx to confront the reality. Now he proposes to marry with Kate and will go to medical school if his aunt wishes from him. In the same way Will Barrett of *The Last Gentleman* tries to understand the past in order to get relieved from its influence. But his amnesia wipes out the past that he tries to confront. Will's final confrontation with the past occurs when he stands before his father's house where his childhood memories return to him. Will is able to learn from those memories that his father was suffering from the romantic cynicism revealed in his reading of Arnold's, *Dover Beach* and his listening to the Brahm's. He acquires the knowledge of the past and on its basis judges that his father was wrong to choose to death.

In *Love in the Ruins* Dr. Tom More tries to come to terms with the past related to the deaths of his daughter and wife. He heightens that past into a particular myth of death and loss as it is unbearable for him. But his "return" to the past, to the memory of Samantha's unshakable faith pulls him out of his role of mythmaker and revives his faith. Lancelot Lamar of

Lancelot also tries to understand his personal history because, he thinks, it contains clues to the present. His attempt to organize the scattered and fragmented pieces of the past is his attempt to recover the clue. After recounting the past without any regret, Lancelot decides to pattern his future on Southern code. He rejects the present age and the Catholic faith while starting a new society in that old womblike seat of Southern glory and defeat, the Shenandoah Valley. Lancelot's new society will be based on the codes of courtesy and chivalry by which, he believes, noble men of the past acted. Will Barrett of *The Second Coming*, too, is engaged in assessing the meanings of memories of the past. He tries to understand the past through memories that visit him. Ultimately, Will learns that the vision and the mood of his father are shaped by the Southern stoic in terms of which he has committed suicide and attempted to kill his son. Having gained the knowledge of the past, Will rejects his father's Stoical way to die and thus exorcized the memory of the past. At the end of the novel, we see both Will and Allison continue to converse with their pasts while making plans for the future. Dr. Tom More of *The Thanatos Syndrome* tries to confront the past in order to recover his old faith. The final confrontation occurs when the memory of his daughter's advice returns to him and he gains his old faith back. Although Dr. Tom More begins his new life with his new family, he never leaves his habit of mythmaking. His obsession with the Stedmann history continues.

In the same way, as Percy's fictitious characters, Foote's fictitious characters, too, are preoccupied with the past, but most often it is the past of the region. The past they are preoccupied with is not a burden to them but a heritage, a pattern to be lived by. Foote's characters are inclined to imagine and interpret their existence in terms of romance of the Old South. Hugh Bart of *Tournament* does the same; he is governed by an obsession with the past, specifically with the grand style of the region. The past style and manner become the main concern in his life. He always maintains the air of gentility and when he notices he has dropped it, he regains it immediately. His attending the games or tournaments—

hunting, shooting, cards—is the part of the pattern of life. The other character in the novel Cassendale Tarfeller tries to live by the code of chivalry and challenges his adversary for a duel. To Tarfeller, the duel is to be conducted in a manner described by the elder Dumas or Walter Scott. Luther Eustis of *Follow Me Down* is obsessed with the region's religious past. Having spent his childhood in the company of his grandfather, the Civil War Veteran who had lost his arm at Shiloh, Eustis wants to have a male heir to continue the heroic tradition of the family. As there is no male child that he gets from his wife, Eustis turns to religion. He is dominated by a desire to follow the letter of the Holy Word. He tries to live by the past protestant morality while living in the present of loose morals represented by Beulah.

The major characters in *Love in a Dry Season* are either obsessively preoccupied with past or simply just neglect it. Major Malcolm Barcroft is that character who is principally preoccupied with the heroic past of his family. Born during Reconstruction and nurtured on the lore of Confederate heroism, the Major wants to prove himself as a military man. Even after he retires with the rank of Major, he plays the role of military hero to the hilt. History is internalized in the mind of the Major. On the other side, Amy and Jeff Carruthers are those characters who have lost their moorings in both history and tradition. Their marital relations are devoid of the traditional values and love. The Southern characters, who are the narrators too, of *Shiloh* are preoccupied with the region's past. Their frame of mind is shaped by the region's past of romance and chivalry and at the same time they feel presence of their personal as well as a European past. Metcalfe who represents Southerners is obsessed with his personal past. He recollects images of his mother whom he knows only from a painting. He feels the grip of a European past on the minds of the Southern military men who plan the battle order after Napoleon's Waterloo order. In *September September*, too, the white set of characters act out the past while living in the present. They are obsessed with the region's past in which the blacks are exploited for white man's greed. To fulfill their personal greed, the white characters kidnap a black boy of a wealthy black family for a huge ransom. The black set of characters, particularly Eben and Martha, on the other hand struggle to confront the unwritten code and tradition in order to get relieved from that.

The character's stance toward history as heritage, as pattern in Foote's novels turns out a malady, a flaw in their character causing suffering and perhaps bringing about their fall. At the same time, the character's lack of sense of the past and the tradition is also an illness. Devoid of the sense of the past and the tradition, Foote's characters are confused about the essence of their lives, hence are ill. Moreover, the characters in Foote's novels do not try to cure the malady or overcome the flaw in their character, rather they prefer to live by it. It is evident in the major characters in all the novels by Foote. In *Tournament* Hugh Bart suffers from the cultural illness embodied in his preoccupation with the grand style. In a sense, he attempts to imagine his existence in terms of romance of the Old South. The grand style proves to be the barriers that thickened around him making him unable to work. It becomes the source of his isolation from his family as he attends the tournaments away from home. Bart's illness turns out a flaw when he sells the land upon his seeing his son's inability to assume the responsibility of the heritage and brings about his fall. Even during the period of his misfortune, Bart's preoccupation with tournaments, specially poker, continues. He does not ponder so much on his fall as he does on the problem how to link different episodes of his past life into a whole. Bart's fellow Southerner, Cassendale Tarfeller also suffers from the malady of romance of the Old South. His attempt to live by the code of chivalry without understanding it, is an illness. He tries to follow the romantic convention not willingly but upon his wife's insistence, consequently he is killed in the duel as he is not prepared for it.

Luther Eustis of *Follow Me Down* is a sick man indeed. His intense preoccupation with the South's religious past generates in him a sense of guilt which is judged by his lawyer Nowell Parker as a fanaticism, a form of insanity. He kills

Beulah because he feels guilty which is accounted for his craziness. Only an insane person can love a girl intensely and kill her at the same time. Eustis does not regret the consequence of his worshipping the past rather he mutely faces that. Eustis's insanity, in a sense, represents the disease of the entire Southern culture. Beulah, the victim, too, suffers from the illness different from that of Eustis's. Her disease is loose morals opposed to the moral certainty of the traditional past. Major Malcolm Barcroft of *Love in a Dry Season* is mentally sick by the real sense of the word. His romantic obsession with the heroic ideals of his family past reaches to the level of insanity. He is in turn frustrated, sadistic, ridiculous and cold-hearted. His behavior toward his daughters and society is not that of a sane man but of an insane person. Consequently, the daughters are afraid of him and the society is hostile toward him. Even his regular barber Sam Marino feels that something is wrong with the house of the Major. The Major's sickness becomes the cause of the failure of his relationship with his daughters and society. However, the Major prefers to be a soldier fighting a Civil War battle in his mind. The Major's reverence for the military tradition, on the other hand, lends him a courteous manner which is lacking in other characters like Harley Drew, Amy and Jeff Carruthers.

Amy and Jeff Carruthers of the same novel *Love in a Dry Season* suffer from modern sickness of lack of values in husband-wife relationship. Having no sense of the history and tradition, the lives of these characters have lost their essence. Jeff prefers to play the role of a voyeur rather than of a husband and Amy desires to be promiscuous rather than Southern belle of the past. The Southern men in *Shiloh* are, in Metcalfe's father's words, sick of an old malady, i.e. romantic idealism by Walter Scott and Dumas, and misplaced chivalry. Though Metcalfe's father is conscious of the malady of Southern men, he himself is an incurable romantic. He poses himself as a realist and straight thinker, but, as Metcalfe says, he was highly romantic man. Metcalfe's awareness of his father's malady does not help him, since he cannot save himself from that malady. Metcalfe's dedication to the romantic warrior Forrest is a sign of his suffering from that old malady. The other Southern character in the novel Luther Dade suffers from romantic idealism that brings him into the battle of Shiloh. For Foote, the Southerners' obsession with the romantic idealism leads them into the Civil War and defeat afterwards. There is no sign at all in the novel of the Southern men's having been cured of the old malady. Though Metcalfe comments on his father's incurable romanticism, he prefers to live by the way his father lived.

The white set of characters in *September September* suffer from the illness attributed to them in the South. Their attempt to retain in the present the old way of white people's living off of the labor of the black community is a symptom of their sickness of mind. The white characters' attempt to live by the past brings about their fall, yet they do not mean to abandon this form of living anywhere in the novel. Only the black set of characters abandon the code that governs the racial relationship in the South.

To wind up the conclusion, I can say that the novels of both Walker Percy and Shelby Foote study the mind of Southern men in relation with the history that has shaped it. For that matter, these two writers explore the individual consciousness of the protagonists where history is always present. Percy tends to be more directly philosophical in his treatment of the Southern mind. He employs the existential terms, particularly from Kierkegaard's existential philosophy, for the better approach to the Southern character. This technique makes Percy's novels the novels of ideas. Foote, on the other hand, does not perceive the Southern mind from the philosophical point of view. His treatment of the Southern mind is simple but strategic. He studies the Southern characters in a particular historical context which affects them very much. Foote's novels turn out the novels of character study. Although these two contemporary writers of the South differ in their technique, their perceptions of the Southern mind is almost congenial.

Bibliography

[A] PRIMARY SOURCES

Foote, Shelby. *Tournament*. 2nd edn. Birmingham, Alabama: Summa Publications, 1987.

———. *Follow Me Down*. New York: Random House, 1978.

———. *Love in a Dry Season*. New York: Random House, 1979.

———. *Shiloh*. New York: The Dial Press, 1952.

———. *September September*. New York: Random House, 1977.

Percy, Walker. *The Moviegoer*. New York: The Noonday Press, 1967.

———. *The Last Gentleman*. New York: Farrar, Straus and Giroux, 1966.

———. *Love in the Ruins*. New York: Farrar, Straus and Giroux, 1971.

———. *Lancelot*. New York: Farrar, 1977.

———. *The Second Coming*. New York: Farrar, Straus and Giroux, 1980.

———. *The Thanatos Syndrome*. New York: Farrar, Straus and Giroux, 1987.

[B] SECONDARY SOURCES

(i) Critical Books

Allen, William Rodney. *Walker Percy: A Southern Wayfarer*. Jackson and London: UP. of Mississippi, 1986.

Bloom, Harold, ed. *Robert Penn Warren's All the Kings Men*. New York: Chelsea House Publishers, 1987.

Bohner, Charles H. *Robert Penn Warren*. New York: Twayne Publishers, 1964.

Brooks, Cleanth. *William Faulkner: The Yoknapatawpha Country*. Baton Rouge and London: Louisiana State UP., 1990.

Broughton, Panthea Reid, ed. *The Art of Walker Percy: Strategems for Being*. Baton Rouge: Louisiana State UP., 1979.

Butterfield, Herbert. *The Historical Novel: An Essay*. Cambridge: Cambridge UP., 1924.

Cash, W.J. *The Mind of the South*. New York: Alfred A. Knopf, 1941.

Cleopatra, Sr. *The Novels of Robert Penn Warren*. New Delhi: Associated Publishing House, 1985.

Coles, Robert. *Walker Percy: An American Search*. Boston: Little, Brown, 1979.

Davidson, Donald. *Southern Writers in the Modern World*. Athens: U of Georgia P, 1958.

Desmond, John F. *Risen Sons: Flannery O' Connor's Vision of History*. Athens and London: The U of Georgia P, 1987.

——, ed. *A Still Moment: Essays On the Art of Eudora Welty*. Metuchen, N.J. and London: The Scarecrow Press, 1978.

Devenport, F.G., Jr. *The Myth of Southern History: Historical Consciousness in Twentieth-Century Literature*. Nashville: Vanderbilt UP., 1967.

Dunn, Joe P. and Howard L. Preston, eds. *The Future of the South: A Historical Perspective for the Twenty-First Century*. U of Illinois P, 1991.

Eaton, Clement. *The Wanning of the Old South Civilization*. New York: Pegasus, 1969.

Feeley, Sister Kathleen, S.S.N.D., *Flannery O' Connor: Voice of the Peacock*. New Brunswick, New Jersey: Rutgers UP., 1972.

Gester, Patrick and Nicholas Cords, eds. *Myth and Southern History*. Chicago: Rand Mc Nally College Publishing Company, 1974.

Gossman, Lionel. *Between History and Literature*. Cambridge: Harward UP., 1990.

Gretlund, John Nordby and Karl-Henz Westarp, eds. *Walker Percy: Novelist and Philosopher*. Jackson and London: UP. of Mississippi, 1991.

Gross, Harvey. *The Contrived Corridor: History and Fatality in Modern Literature*. Ann Arbor: U of Michigan P., 1971.

Hardy, John Edward. *The Fiction of Walker Percy*. Urbana and Chicago: U of Illinois P., 1987.

Henderson, Harry B., III. *Versions of the Past: The Historical Imagination in American Fiction*. New York: Oxford UP., 1974.

Hobson, Linda W. *Understanding Walker Percy*. Columbia, South Carolina: U of S. Carolina P., 1988.

Hoffman, Frederick J. *The Art of Southern Fiction: A Study of Some Modern Novelists*. Carbondale and Edwardsville: Southern Illinois UP., 1967.

Holman, C. Hugh. *Three Modes of Southern Fiction*. Athens: U of Georgia P., 1966.

———. *The Immoderate Past: The Southern Writer and History*. Athens: The U of Geogia P., 1977.

Howland, Mary D. *The Gift of the Other: Gabriel Marcel's Concept of Intersubjectivity in Walker Percy's Novels*. Pittsburg, Pennsylvania: Duquesne UP., 1990.

Kreyling, Michael. *Eudora Welty's Achievement of Order*. Baton Rouge and London: Louisiana State UP., 1980.

Lawson, Lewis A. *Following Percy: Essays on Walker Percy's Work*. Troy, New York: The Whitson Publishing Company, 1988.

Lehan, Richard. *A Dangerous Crossing: French Literary Existentialism and the Modern American Novel.* Carbondale and Edwardsville: Illinois UP., 1973.

Linderberger, Herbert. *The History in Literature: On Value, Genre, Institutions.* New York: Columbia UP., 1990.

Lively, Robert A. *Fiction Fights the Civil War: An Unfinished Chapter in the Literary History of the American People.* Chapel Hill: The U of North Carolina P., 1957.

Luschei, Martin. *The Sovereign Wayfarer: Walker Percy's Diagnosis of the Malaise.* Baton Rouge: Louisiana State UP., 1972.

Mac Kethan, Lucinda. *The Dream of Arcady: Place and Time in Southern Literature.* Baton Rouge: Louisiana State UP., 1980.

Martin, Carter. *The True Country: Themes in the Fictions of Flannery O' Connor.* Nashville: Vanderbilt UP., 1970.

Mc Cormick, John, *American Literature 1919-1932: A Comparative History.* London: Routledge and Kegan Paul, 1971.

Miner, Ward L. *The World of William Faulkner.* New York: Grove Press, 1952.

Morse, Jonathan. *Word By Word: Language of Memory.* Ithaca: Carnell UP., 1990.

Nadel, Alan. *Invisible Criticism: Ralf Ellison and the American Canon.* Iowa City: U of Iowa P., 1988.

Nakadate, Neil, ed. *Robert Penn Warren: Critical Perspective.* Kentucky: The UP. of Kentucky, 1981.

O'Meally, Robert. *The Craft of Ralf Ellison.* Cambridge, Massachusetts: Harvard UP., 1980.

———. *New Essays on Invisible Man.* Cambridge: Cambridge UP., 1988.

Phillips, Robert L. *Shelby Foote: Novelist and Historian.* Jackson: UP. of Mississippi, 1992.

Poteat, Patricia Lewis. *Walker Percy and the Old Modern Age: Reflections on Languages, Arguments and the Telling of*

Stories. Baton Rouge and London: Louisiana State UP., 1985.

Prenshaw, Peggy W. *Eudora Welty: Thirteen Essays*. Jackson: UP. of Mississippi, 1983.

Prescott, Orville. *The Undying Past*. Garden City, New York: Doubleday, 1961.

Reed, John Shelton. *The Enduring South*. Lexington, Massachusetts: Lexington Books, D.C., Heath and Company, 1972.

Rollyson, Carl E., Jr. *Uses of the Past in the Novels of William Faulkner*. Ann Arbor, Michigan: UMI Research Press, 1984.

Rozwence, Edwin C. *Reconstruction in the South: Problems in American Civilization*. Boston: D.C. Heath and Company, 1952.

Rubin, Louis D. and Robert D. Jacob, eds. *Southern Renascence*. Baltimore: The Johns Hopkins Press, 1953.

——. *South: Modern Southern Literature in its Cultural Setting*. Garden City, New York: Doubleday, 1961.

Rubin, Louis D. and C. Hugh Holman, eds. *Southern Literary Studies: Problems and Possibilities*. Chapel Hill: The U of North Carolina P., 1975.

Rubin, Louis D., Jr. *The Writers in the South: Studies in Literary Community*. USA: U of Georgia P., 1972.

——, ed. *The American South: Portrait of Culture*. 2nd ed. Washington: US Information Agency, 1991.

——, ed. *History of Southern Literature*. Baton Rouge and London: Louisiana State UP., 1985.

Savage, Henry, Jr. *Seeds of Time: The Background of Southern Thinking*. New York: Henry Holt and Company, 1959.

Schor, Edith. *Visible Ellison: A Study of Ralf Ellison's Fiction*. London: Greenwood Press, 1993.

Simpson, Lewis P. *The Fable of the Southern Writer*. Baton Rouge and London: Louisiana State UP., 1994.

——. *The Dispossessed Garden: Pastoral and History in Southern Literature*. Athens: U of Georgia P., 1975.

Stephenson, W.H. *A Basic History of the South*. New York: D. Van Nostrand Company, INC., 1959.

Street, James, Jr., ed. *James Street's South*. Garden City, New York: Doubleday and Company, INC., 1955.

Sullivan, Walter. *A Requiem for the Renascence: The State of Fiction in Modern South*. Athens: U of Georgia P., 1976.

Sweeny, Mary K. *Walker Percy and the Postmodern World*. Chicago: Loyola UP., 1987.

Tanner, Tony. *City of Words: American Fiction 1950-1970*. New York: Harper and Row, 1971.

Taylor, Jerome. *In Search of Self: Life, Death and Walker Percy*. Cambridge: Cowley Publication, 1986.

Tharpe, Jac. *Walker Percy*. Boston: Twayne Publishers, 1983.

Turner, W.C. and Lee E. Harding, eds. *Critical Essays of Eudora Welty*. Boston, Massachusetts: G.K. Hal and Co., 1989.

Ungar, Frederick and Lina Mainiero, eds. *Encyclopedia of World Literature in Twentieth Century*. New York: Ungar, 1975.

Vinson, James, ed. *Contemporary Novelists*. 2nd edn. New York: St. Martin's Press, 1976.

Woodward, C. Vann. *The Burden of Southern History*. Rev. edn. Baton Rouge: Louisiana State UP., 1968.

——. *The Future of the Past*. New York, Oxford: Oxford UP., 1989.

Wyatt-Brown, Bertram. *Honor and Violence in the Old South*. New York: Oxford UP., 1986.

Young, Thoman Daniel. *The Past in the Present: A Thematic Study of Modern Southern Fiction*. Baton Rouge and London: Louisiana State UP., 1981.

Zinn, Howard. *The Southern Mystique*. New York: Knopf, 1964.

(ii) Articles

Allen, Harvey. "History and The Novel". *The Atlantic Monthly*, February 1944: 119-21.

Belsches, Alan T. "Life Over Death: The Use Memory in Walker Percy's *The Second Coming*". *The Southern Quarterly* XXIII. 4 (Summer, 1985): 37-47.

Bradbury, John M. "Absurd Insurrection: The Barth-Percy Affair." *South Atlantic Quarterly* LXVIII (Summer, 1969): 319-29.

Brinkmeyer, Robert H., Jr. "Percy's Bludgeon: Message and Narrative Strategy." *The Southern Quarterly* XVIII. 3 (Spring, 1980): 80-89.

Brooks, Cleanth. "The Current State of American Literature." *Southern Review* IX.1 (January, 1973): 273-87.

Brugger, Robert J. "The Mind of Old South: New Views." *Virginia Quarterly Review* LVI (Spring, 1980): 277-95.

Byrd, Scott. "Mysteries and Movies: Walker Percy's College Articles and *The Moviegoer*." *Mississippi Quarterly* XXV. 2 (Spring, 1972): 165-181.

Cashin, Edward J. "History as Mores: Walker Percy's *Lancelot*." *Georgia Review* 31 (1977): 875-80.

Cheney, Brainerd. "Secular Society as Deadly Farce". *Sewanee Review* 75 (Spring, 1967): 345-50.

Chesnick, Eugene. "Novel's Ending and the World's End: The Fiction of Walker Percy." *Hollins Critic* X. 5 (Oct., 1973): 1-11.

Christensen, Jerome C. "Lancelot: Sign for the Times." *The Southern Quarterly* XVIII. 3 (Spring, 1980): 107-120.

Ciuba, Gary M. "*The Moviegoer*: Sign of the Divine Eiron." *Notes on Contemporary Literature* XVII.5 (Nov., 1987): 10-13.

———. "Percy's First Gentleman." *Mississippi Quarterly* LXI. 2 (Spring, 1988): 131-145.

Cleave, Jim Van. "Versions of Percy". *Southern Review* VI. 4 (Oct. 1970): 990-1010.

Daniel, Robert D. "Walker Percy's *Lancelot*: Secular Raving and Religious Silence." *Southern Review* XIV. 1 (Jan., 1978): 186-194.

Davidson, Donald. "Still Rebels, Still Yankees." *American Review* 11. (Nov., 1933): 58-72.

——. "The Class Approach to Southern Problems." *The Southern Review* V. 2 (Autumn, 1939): 261-72.

Desmond, John. "Walker Percy and T.S. Eliot: The Lancelot Andrews Connection." *Southern Review* 22. 3 (Summer, 1986): 465-77.

——. "Love, Sex and Knowledge in Walker Percy's *Lancelot*: A Metaphysical View." *Mississippi Quarterly* 39. 2 (Spring, 1986): 103-109.

——. The Lessons of History: Flannery O'Connor's "Everything that Rises must Converge." *The Flannery O'Connor Bulletin* I (Autumn, 1972): 39-45.

Dowie, William. "Walker Percy: Sensualist Thinker." *Novel* 6. 1 (Fall, 1972): 52-62).

Eubanks, Cecil L "Walker Percy: Eschatology and the Politics of Grace." *The Southern Quarterly* XVII. 3 (Spring, 1980): 121-35.

Fowler, Doreen A. "Answers and Ambiguity in Percy's *The Second Coming. Critique* 23.2 (Winter, 1981-82): 13-23.

Freshney, Pamela. "*The Moviegoer* and *Lancelot*: The Movies as Literary Symbol." *Southern Review* XVII. 4 (Oct., 1982): 71-72.

Fuller, Edmund. "History and the Novelists." *American Scholar* 16.1 (Winter, 1946-47): 113-24.

Gatson, Paul L. "The Revelation of Walker Percy". *Colorado Quarterly* 20. 4 (Spring, 1972): 459-70.

George, P. Garrett. "Talking with Shelby Foote." *Mississippi Quarterly* xxiv . 4 (Fall, 1971): 405-27.

Gray, Richard J. "The American Novelist and American History: A Revaluation of *All the King's Men*." *Journal of American Studies* 3. (1972): 297-300.

——. "The Meanings of History: William Faulkner's *Absalom, Absalom.*" *Dutch Quarterly Review of Anglo-American Letters* 3 (1973): 97-110.

Hardy, John Edward. "Percy and Place: Some Beginnings and Endings." *The Southern Quarterly* xvii. 3 (Spring, 1980): 5-25.

Harrington, Evans. "Interview with Shelby Foote." *The Mississippi Quarterly* xxiv. 4 (Fall, 1971): 349-77.

Heilman, Robert. "The Southern Temper." *Hopkins Review* VI (Fall, 1952): 5-15.

Holley, Joe. "Walker Percy and the Novel of Ultimate Concern." *Southern Review* 65. 3 (Summer, 1980): 225-34.

Johnson, Mark. "*Lancelot*: Percy's Romance." *Southern Literary Journal* 15.2 (Spring, 1983): 19-30.

——. "The Search for Place in Walker Percy's Novels." *Southern Literary Journal* 8.1 (Fall, 1975): 55-81.

Jones, Eric L. "Percy's Parousia." *The Southern Quarterly* XXII. 4 (Summer, 1985): 48-55.

Kermode, Franck. "Novel, History and Type." *Novel* 1 (Spring, 1968): 231-33.

Kissel, Susans. "Walker Percy's 'Conversions'". *Southern Literary Journal* ix. 2 (Spring, 1977): 124 -36.

Knickerbocker, William S. "Asides and Soliloquies." *Sewanee Review* XLII (July-Sept., 1934): 257-60.

Landess, Thomas H. "Southern History and Manhood: Major Themes in the Works of Shelby Foote." *Mississippi Quarterly* xxiv. 4 (Fall, 1971): 321-47.

Lauder, Robert E. "The Catholic Novel and the 'Insider God'". *Commonweal* 101 (25 October, 1974): 78-81.

Lawson, Lewis A. "Walker Percy's Southern Stoic". *Southern Literary Journal* 3.1 (Fall, 1970): 5-31.

——. "Walker Percy's Silent Character." *Mississippi Quarterly* XXXIII . 2 (Spring, 1980): 123-40.

——. "Moviegoing in *The Moviegoer.*" *The Southern Quarterly* XVIII.3 (Spring, 1980): 26-40.

——. "Moviegoing in Percy's *Lancelot.*" *South Central Review* 3.4 (Winter, 1986): 78-94.

Lehan, Richard. "The Way Back: Redemption in the Novels of Walker Percy." *Southern Review* iv. 4 (April, 1968): 306-19.

Maxwell, Robert. "Walker Percy's Fancy." *Minnesota Review* 7.3 (1967): 231-37.

Milton, Edith. "Seven Recent Novels." *Yale Review* 67. 2 (Dec., 1977): 260-71.

Morse, J. Mitchell. "Fiction Chronicle." *Hudson Review* 24 (Autumn, 1971): 526-540.

O'Brien, William James. "Walker Percy's *Lancelot*: A Beatrician Visit to the Region of the Dead." *Southern Humanities Review* 15 (Spring, 1981): 153-64.

Oliver, Bill. "A Manner of Speaking: Percy's *Lancelot.*" *The Southern Literary Journal* xv. 2 (Spring, 1983): 7-18.

Owsley, Frank L. "The Pillars of Agrarianism." *American Review* IV (March, 1935): 529-47.

Pearson, Michael. "The Double Bondage of Racism in Walker Percy's Fiction." *Mississippi Quarterly* XLI. 4 (Fall, 1988): 479-95.

Potter, David M. "The Enigma of the South." *Yale Review* LI (October, 1961): 142-51.

Ranson, John Crowe. "The South-Old or New?" *Sewanee Review* xxxvi (April, 1928): 139-47.

——. "The Aesthetics of Regionalism." *American Review* II (January, 1934): 290-310.

Simpson, Lewis P. "The Southern Aesthetic of Memory." *Tulane Studies in English* 23 (1978): 207-27.

Smith, Frank E. "The Emerging South." *The Virginia Quarterly Review* 41. 2 (Spring, 1965): 161-75.

Sullivan, Walter. "The Insane and the Indifferent: Walker Percy and Others." *Sewanee Review* 86.1 (Winter, 1978): 153-59.

Tate, Allen. "A View of the Old South." *American Review* II (Feb., 1934): 411-32.

Taylor, Alastair Mac Donald. "The Historical Novel: As A Source in History." *Sewanee Review* XLVI (Oct., 1938): 459-79.

Taylor, Lewis J., Jr. "Walker Percy and the Self." *Commonweal* 100 (10 May, 1974): 233-36.

Tindall, George B. "The Benighted South: Origins of a Modern Image." *Virginia Quarterly Review* XL (Spring, 1964): 281-94.

Tourtellot, Arthur B. "History and the Historical Novel: Where Fact and Fancy Meet and Part." *The Saturday Review* XXII. 18 (24 August, 1940): 3-4, 16.

Tremonte, Colleen M. "The Poet-Prophet and Feminine Capability in Walker Percy's *The Second Coming.*" *The Mississippi Quarterly* XLLIII. 2 (Spring, 1990): 173-81.

Vance, Rupert B. "Beyond the Fleshpots: The Coming Culture Crisis in the South." *Virginia Quarterly Review* XLI (Spring, 1965): 217-30.

Vauthier, Simone. "The Symmetrical Design: The Structural Patterns of *Love in a Dry Season.*" *The Mississippi Quarterly* XXIV. 4 (Fall, 1971): 379-403.

Walter, James. "Spinning and Spieling: A Trick and a Kick in Walker Percy's *The Moviegoer.*" *Southern Review* 16. 3 (July 1980): 574-90.

Welty, Eudora. "Some Notes on Time in Fiction." *The Mississippi Quarterly* 26 (Fall, 1978): 483-92.

(iii) Reviews

Cantinella, Joseph. Rev. of *Love in the Ruins. Saturday Review* 54 (15 May, 1971): 42-43.

Cournos, John. Rev. of *Follow Me Down. Saturday Review* xxxiii (2 Sep., 1950): 31.

Gaither, Frances. "Dry-Rot In Dixie." Rev. of *Love in a Dry Season,* by Shelby Foote. *New York Times Book Review,* 23 Sept., 1951: 26.

Gardener, John. Rev. of *Lancelot. New York Times Book Review,* 20 Feb., 1977: 1, 16.

Krim, Seymour. Rev. of *Follow Me Down. New York Times Book Review,* 9 July, 1950: 20.

Larder, Susan. Rev. of *Lancelot. New Yorker* 53 (2 May, 1977): 141-43.

Malin, Irving. "Cross Purposes." Rev. of *Lancelot*, by Walker Percy. *Virginia Quarterly Review* 53. 3 (Summer 1977): 568-71.

Massie, Robert. Rev. of *The Moviegoer. New York Times Book Review,* 28 May, 1961: 30.

Mc Cleary, William. Rev. of *The Moviegoer. Library Journal* 86 (15 May, 1961): 1905.

Mc Millan, George. "The Hero Is A Battle." Rev. of *Shiloh*, by Shelby Foote. *New York Times Book Review* 6 April, 1952: 6.

Pine, John C. Rev. of *The Last Gentleman. Library Journal* 91. 11 (1 June 1966): 2877.

Rolo, Charles. "Men Fighting." Rev. of *Shiloh*, by Shelby Foote. *Atlantic* 189. 5 (May, 1952): 81-82.

Taylor, Mark. Rev. of *Love in the Ruins. Commonweal* 95 (29 Oct., 1971): 118-19.

Wiehe, Janet. Rev. of *The Second Coming. Library Journal* 105 (July, 1980): 1541-42.

Wilkie, Brian. Rev. of *The Last Gentleman. Commonweal* 84. 19 (19 August, 1966): 537-39.